# love in their hearts

# love in their hearts

## A Celebration of Animal Emotions and a Guide to Compassionate Action

**Marc Bekoff & Jeff Campbell**

**Foreword by Dr. Jane Goodall**

Love in Their Hearts: A Celebration of Animal Emotions and a Guide to Compassionate Action


ISBN (paperback): 978-1-968919-30-6
ISBN (ebook): 978-1-968919-31-3

ARMINLEAR

Armin Lear Press, Inc.
215 W Riverside Drive, #4362
Estes Park, CO 80517

Cover photo captions:
Front cover: top, Gombe, a ten-month-old chimpanzee, the grandson of Gremlin—a chimpanzee studied by Jane Goodall, Gombe Stream National Park, Tanzania; bottom, a female red fox and her kits, Wyoming.
Inside front cover: top, Jane Goodall working in her tent in Gombe National Park; bottom, a common bottlenose dolphin.
Back cover: Bear 399 and her cubs, Grand Teton National Park, Wyoming.
Inside back cover: African elephants, Amboseli National Park, Kenya.

Cover photo credits:
Front cover, back cover, inside back cover: Photos courtesy of Thomas D. Mangelsen, Images of Nature
Inside front cover, top: Photo by Hugo van Lawick
Inside front cover, bottom: Photo © 2025 maddalenabearzi/OCS (under NOAA permit)

***We dedicate this book to Dr. Jane Goodall, whose astonishing life was dedicated to science, education, advocacy, humanitarianism, hope, and peace.***

**Where to find the source notes:**

This book is based on lots of scientific research, and stories are told firsthand or come from published sources. The source notes are available at marcbekoff.com/love-in-their-hearts:

# contents

**foreword** i

**introduction** 1

**1 good day, sunshine:** Joy, Delight, and Playfulness 11
- Field Notes: Paidia Plays with Her Cubs 13
- Dogs Just Wanna Have Fun 16
- Wildlife Guide: Animals at Play 22
- Jokers of the Sea 29
- Get Started: Anyone Can Do Citizen Science 33

**2 lean on me:** Empathy and Compassion 39
- Jethro and Bunny 40
- Taking Care of the Flock 44
- Job Application: Rat Lifeguard at the Rodent Pool 46
- A Herd Leader Submits 49
- Learning to Read Signs 53
- Get Started: Humane Education—Compassion in the Classroom 55

**3 oh, what a wonderful world:** Curiosity, Wonder, and Awe 59
- Making Friends with an Alien 60
- Wanted by the ZBI 66
- The Great Rain, the Mighty Waterfall 70
- Get Started: Unleashing Your Pet 75

**4 under pressure:** Fear, Anxiety, Pain, and Worry 77
- Cow #6490 78
- Wildlife Guide: Stranger Things 84
- Jasper: The Spokes-Bear for Forgiveness and Hope 88
- Get Started: Our Compassion Footprint—Who and What We Eat and Buy 93

**5 at home with the blues:** Sadness, Grief, and Depression 97
- Elephant Funerals 98
- Wildlife Guide: Animals in Mourning 103
- A Sorrow Beyond Tears 108
- Captive Dolphin Depression Syndrome 111
- Of Singing and Sadness 117
- Get Started: The Problem with Zoos and Waterparks 120

**6 you're no good:** Frustration, Anger, Disgust, and Contempt 123
Want a Nut 124
On Trial: The People Vs. Octopuses 127
Don't Diss the Matriarch 132
Get Started: Defining Animals—Laws, Regulations, and Rights 137

**7 i hung my head:** Pride, Jealousy, Guilt, and Shame 141
Field Notes: Penguin Pranksters 142
No Quid Pro Quo 145
Sorry Is the Hardest Word 148
Get Started: Putting Out the Welcome Mat—Wildlife in Our Backyards 150

**8 you've got a friend in me:** Love, Friendship, Trust, and Devotion 155
An Elephant's Kiss 156
Field Notes: Grooming David Greybeard 159
One of the Herd 164
Mother Bear: Queen of the Tetons 170
Get Started: Compassionate Conservation—Who Lives, Who Dies, and Why 178

**9 help! i need somebody:** Altruism and Gratitude 183
Cat Versus Dog 184
Dolphin Versus Shark 186
It's a Bird, It's a Plane, It's … Humpback Whales! 190
A Knotty Question 194
Part of the Family 200
Get Started: Rewilding in the Anthropocene 204

**afterword:** The Ten Trusts 207

**acknowledgments** 210

**select bibliography** 211

**get started resources** 214

**index** 218

**about the authors** 226

# foreword

I am very happy to write this Foreword for *Love in Their Hearts* by my friend Marc Bekoff and coauthor Jeff Campbell. I turned ninety in April 2024, and I feel my mission in life is to give people hope, especially young people. It is all too easy to get discouraged over the struggles facing our world, to feel hopeless, and this moving, important book is filled with hope. It combines scientific findings with wonderful stories about the rich emotional lives of animals that will inspire readers to learn more—to keep wondering about the inner lives of all beings—while also empowering readers to take action on behalf of animals, nature, and our planet.

Jane Goodall enjoying nature, Nebraska, 2010.
Photo courtesy of Thomas D. Mangelsen, Images of Nature.

I think this is the most exciting time ever for anybody wanting to study animals and animal behavior. We're learning things that nobody would have believed even ten years ago. People need to understand that animal intelligence and sentience don't just stop with apes and dolphins and elephants. Highly intelligent octopuses have "brains" in all eight arms that can act independently. Bees learn and like to play. Chickens make lifelong friends. Cows grieve separation from their children. These and many other species are brought to life in this engaging book.

Throughout my childhood I was fascinated with animals of all sorts—I watched them, learned from them, and loved them. My wonderful family welcomed three successive cats, two guinea pigs (whom I harnessed and took for walks), one golden hamster (who decided to live in the sofa), one canary and one budgerigar (both were allowed to fly freely in the house), and two rescued tortoises.

Jane and her childhood friend, Rusty. Photo from the Jane Goodall Institute/ courtesy of the Goodall family.

My most special relationship was with Rusty, an extraordinarily intelligent mixed-breed dog who entered my life when I was ten and became my constant companion. I've never known another dog like him. He didn't even belong to us. He belonged to a hotel down the road. He used to come along, bark outside our house at six in the morning, get let in, stay with us all morning, go home for lunch, come back, and leave when we put him out at ten. The hotel knew; they couldn't have cared less. It was as though he was sent to me.

When I was ten years old, I bought a small secondhand book called *Tarzan of the Apes*. I fell passionately in love with that glorious lord of the jungle, but what did he do? He married the wrong Jane! That's when I decided I would go to Africa when I grew up, live with wild animals, and write books about them. Of course, everybody laughed. But I had this amazing, supportive mother. And she said if you really want to do this, then you have to work really hard and take advantage of every opportunity, and if you don't give up, you'll find a way. I share that advice with young people around the world.

In 1960, after I saved up to go to Africa to stay with a friend, I was offered the extraordinary opportunity to learn about the chimpanzees of Gombe National Park in Tanzania. I had not been to university (we could not afford it), so I did what came naturally—observed and recorded everything I saw, writing in small notebooks with pen or pencil as I had throughout my childhood. It was fortunate that I was patient, for during the first four months the chimps fled whenever they saw the strange white ape who had appeared so suddenly in their midst. The first individual to lose his fear I named David Greybeard, which is a story that Marc and Jeff share.

After a year, I was sent by my mentor to Cambridge University to work toward a PhD in ethology. First thing, I was told that I'd done everything wrong. Chimps couldn't be named, they should be numbered. You couldn't talk about their personalities. You couldn't talk about them having minds capable of solving problems. You certainly couldn't talk about them having emotions. And I was told that scientists could not have empathy with their "subjects" because then they could not be objective. Fortunately, thanks to the great teacher I had as a child, I knew that in these respects those erudite scientists were quite wrong. My teacher was my dog Rusty!

When I submitted my first scientific paper for publication in *Nature*, the editor crossed out everywhere I had written "he" or "she" and substituted "it." The chimpanzees were even to be deprived of their gender! Where I had written "who," they substituted "which." I crossed out each *it* and *which* and underlined every *he* and *she* and *who.* And that was published.

In 1991, I founded the youth action program Roots & Shoots. Our goal is to inspire compassion for animals, people, and the environment and to empower young people to solve problems in their own communities. I met Marc a few years after that, and he initially helped with Roots & Shoots events in Boulder, Colorado. In 2002, we coauthored the book *The Ten Trusts*, about caring for animals. Ever since, we've continued to grow Roots & Shoots—Marc is a Roots & Shoots "ambassador"—while occasionally writing together. We share many values, and of course, we're both ethologists.

People sometimes ask what I would most like to be remembered for. I say two things. One is how my work with chimpanzees—because they are so biologically as well as behaviorally our closest relatives—helped to break down the sharp line that science had drawn between humans and the rest of the animal kingdom. We are indeed part of and not separated from other animals. The other is starting Roots & Shoots and getting young people to take action. Today, the program exists in over seventy countries and involves children from kindergarten through university. Through the programs, young people choose projects they are passionate about that will improve the world for everyone. Whenever I get discouraged, the commitment of young people to affect positive change gives me hope.

Everywhere I go, and I still travel constantly, my message is the same: Every individual makes an impact on the planet—every day. So choose wisely and turn knowledge into action. So many people feel helpless because they are overwhelmed by the problems facing us around the world. An individual cannot change the world, but everyone can make a difference in their own community, such as by volunteering at an animal shelter or joining a group that collects trash, plants trees, and so on.

You can't do everything, but the thing that you decide to do—give it all you've got.

—**Jane Goodall,** PhD, DBE,<br>
UN Messenger of Peace, Founder of the Jane Goodall Institute<br>
December 2024

Jane Goodall by Patrick McDonnell.


**Authors' Note:** On October 1, 2025, Jane Goodall died in her sleep of natural causes. She was ninety-one, had been awarded the US Presidential Medal of Freedom in January 2025, and was in the middle of a speaking tour. "Dr. Jane," as countless people around the world called her, was mourned globally, and continues to be, by millions of people who were deeply touched by her tireless, heartfelt commitment to make the world a better place for all beings. Her impact is apparent in this book, which features her compassionate views on animal well-being and her dedication to humane education, including the Jane Goodall Institute's Roots & Shoots program. To experience what made Jane so beloved, read *Jane Goodall at 90*. Edited by Marc and his colleague Dr. Koen Margodt, this book celebrated Jane's ninetieth birthday by collecting ninety original essays by people whose hearts were touched and lives transformed by Jane.

# introduction

Bear 399 and three cubs, Pilgrim Creek Road, Grand Teton National Park, Wyoming.
Photo courtesy of Thomas D. Mangelsen, Images of Nature.

Anyone who's ever lived with a dog knows that dogs rarely hide their feelings. Say the words *dinner* or *walk* and they transform: Through their expressive behavior, with every quivering fiber of their shaggy being, they radiate pure joy and excitement.

And when dogs don't like something, their behavior tells us that, too—from their sad "hang dog" expressions to their anxious barks whenever the doorbell rings.

Other animals can be harder to read, especially those we aren't familiar with and who don't look like us. An orca, a magpie, a goldfish, a bee, an octopus: What might they be feeling and experiencing?

Even when we can't tell, we know *something* is going on behind each mysterious gaze. Through research, we've learned that countless animals are sentient, or capable of feeling. In fact, our world is one big ocean of emotion—from skies to seas, from fields to forests. We can't yet say that every species is sentient, but we have yet to confirm any species that isn't.

This book is a celebration and exploration of the emotional lives of animals—including humans, since we are also animals. It tells stories that show how love and many other feelings beat in the hearts of Earth's creatures and how these shared emotions inspire our connection to and love for animals.

This book is also a call to action. We have much more to learn about the inner lives of nonhuman animals, and what we learn must influence how we treat and care for them. This book shares what we know about animal emotions (based on current research), shows how to observe and recognize animal emotions (featuring those who do it for a living), and asks the most important question: Given what we know, what should we do?

As everyone knows, our world is troubled. The planet is threatened by climate change, pollution, and our gigantic human footprint, and far too many animals in our care don't experience enough caring.

We believe and hope that knowing how deeply and profoundly animals feel will inspire people, in whatever ways they can, to make the lives of animals better.

## Celebrating Animals and Celebrating People

The heart of this book is its collection of animal stories, which embodies the universality of emotions. Each chapter focuses on a group of closely related emotions and tells a few of many possible stories. It would take a ten-volume encyclopedia to include every species and every emotion. This is only a sample.

Further, these stories aren't meant to "prove" animals have feelings. We know they do, based on solid science and extensive research. (For this book's source notes, visit https://marcbekoff.com/love-in-their-hearts.) Rather, through stories, we hope to bring those emotions to life. Some stories are playful; some dramatic and heartbreaking. A few are even tongue-in-cheek: Through absurd humor, they highlight important messages. But all the stories describe true events. Many come from renowned scientists, and each reflects the current state of animal research.

Ultimately, our goal is to paint a vivid, fun, moving portrait of Earth's diverse family of sentient beings.

The stories also celebrate the people who research and work on behalf of animals. Many are ethologists. Among the various goals of ethology is understanding the inner lives of animals (including how behavior evolves) and how animals experience the world from their own perspectives.

This isn't easy. Each species and each individual is different. In this book's Wildlife Guides, we share anecdotes about a variety of species to show how related emotions are expressed—sometimes in unique behaviors, and sometimes in strikingly common ones.

Observing wild animals in nature, called fieldwork, can also be thrilling. In entries titled Field Notes, we sketch portraits of ethologists in action. To learn about animals, we can't just observe from a distance; getting close and developing relationships, or at least familiarity, with wild animals is essential.

Putting people in the picture is important for another reason. Emotions don't exist in a vacuum, and a person observing animals experiences their own feelings and reactions. All the people in these stories felt empathy and even compassion for animals, and these feelings sometimes sparked intuitive understandings of behavior. Scientists are trained to be objective, but that doesn't mean they lack feelings.

Dolphin researcher Maddalena Bearzi says, when something unexpected or extraordinary happens, "I put my dry scientific objectivity on hold in favor of the empathy of the moment."

A compassionate connection to animals often begins in childhood. In this book's Childhood Inspiration sidebars, six people, including Maddalena, share their stories of how animals impacted them as kids and inspired them to continue caring for and even studying animals and nature as adults. We hope these stories, and this book, do the same for readers. Becoming a close, curious observer of animals—sitting quietly in a park, watching animals do their thing, feeling part of nature—helps inspire a desire to learn more and do more to protect our world. As Jane Goodall shares in her Foreword, and as Marc shares below, many animal scientists and advocates began their careers as children who simply loved animals.

## Getting Started: Why Animal Emotions Matter

Recognizing that animals have emotions is important because their feelings matter. Their emotions absolutely matter to them, and they should matter to us. Most animals are sentient beings who experience the ups and downs of life, and we must respect this when we interact with them. This includes the animals we live with, care for, and love—those we call our companions. It includes the billions of other domesticated animals in industry and society—those who provide us with food and clothing, entertain us, and are used in research labs. And it includes wild animals, who struggle to share our ever-crowded world.

Compassion starts with empathy, which means understanding and feeling the emotions of others, including imagining their point of view. We often need that sense of connection to inspire action, and that's another reason for the way this book is written. Stories can help us experience what others are feeling and inspire the desire to help. And nonhuman animals need all the help they can get.

Marc often writes about the "empathy gap" that exists between us and other animals. Overcoming this gap is one of our biggest challenges today, for the sake of nonhuman animals, the world, and ourselves. A few years ago, Marc gave a talk about animal emotions in Denver, Colorado, and a thirteen-year-old middle-schooler named Monika asked if he thought we were a "failed mammal" because of the harm we've caused to nonhuman animals and the environment. Marc was shocked by her question, and it still haunts him. Humans often have a superiority complex. We think we're better and smarter than other animals, and that arrogance can lead to disrespect that justifies the harm we cause.

The antidote to this is teaching and practicing tolerance and developing an ethic of caring and respect for all life. We share with all creatures a bountiful, beautiful, diverse planet, one full of grandeur and awe. We shouldn't take this for granted. Instead, we must do everything possible to protect and preserve it so future generations enjoy what we have.

Marc is an award-winning ethologist who often gives talks, and when he speaks with young people, they often ask him what they can do. In this book, we suggest many actions anyone can take—including simply learning more about animals. That is the focus of each chapter's Get Started section. These raise a few key issues, and they focus in particular on how young people might help.

Throughout, we also highlight examples of young people doing research and taking action. As Marc and Jane have learned through the Jane Goodall Institute's Roots & Shoots program, one cause for genuine optimism about our future is the inspiration of young people as they dedicate themselves to being the change they want to see.

## Minding Animals

Marc is a widely recognized expert in animal emotions and a tireless advocate on behalf of all nonhuman beings. For over fifty years, he has worked as both an ethologist and a cognitive ethologist (focusing on animal minds). He's studied a range of species, but particularly canids: wolves, coyotes, and domestic dogs (who share a wolf ancestor). He's a former college professor; he's published more than thirty books on animals; and he's received many awards for his scientific research and animal advocacy.

Jeff is a book editor and writer who has helped edit Marc's books for twenty years, including Marc's groundbreaking work *The Emotional Lives of Animals*. Like most people, he grew up loving his family's dogs and cats and is forever hoping to meet wild animals in the wild, but his collaborations with Marc inspired him to write about animals. Jeff has authored three books of animal science for young adults: *Daisy to the Rescue* (about animal emotions), *Last of the Giants* (about conservation), and *Glowing Bunnies!?* (about animal bioengineering).

This is their first cowritten book, and periodically, Marc "takes the mic" to speak directly about his own experience. Below, Marc shares the story of how his innate love of animals as a child inspired who he became as an adult:

## Marc's Story: A Tricycle in Brooklyn

Three-year-old Marc
on his field vehicle, Brooklyn, New York.

My nonlinear journey began in the streets of Brooklyn and went from Antarctica to Grand Teton National Park in Wyoming to Colorado's Rocky Mountains, and beyond. I'm not surprised by where I am today, but it wasn't obvious as my life unfolded.

When I was young, I spent as much time outside as possible, and my tricycle was my "field" vehicle.

My parents told me that, when I was around three, I started asking what animals were thinking and feeling—especially the dogs, squirrels, birds, and ants I met outside our apartment. They said I was constantly "minding animals," and that stuck with me. I even used it as the title for one of my books. To me, it meant two things: I attributed minds to animals, and I was very concerned with how they were treated. I always said we needed to care for them because they couldn't do it for themselves.

We didn't live with a companion animal. My mom was bitten by a dog when she was young and was afraid of them. I had a goldfish buddy, and I used to talk to him as I ate breakfast, wondering what life was like in a small bowl. I told my folks that it wasn't nice to keep him cooped up alone.

I struggled having to go to school and sit inside. Later, I came to think of this as "unwilding," and I "rewilded" myself by spending as much time as I could outside watching, listening to, and smelling my animal neighbors.

When I talked to animals, I felt they heard and understood me. My parents allowed me to do this, but some of the neighbors thought I was fairly wacky. I seemed to have a way with animals. I was told that animals who didn't warm up to others instantly warmed up to me.

Growing up, I always felt closer to nonhumans than to humans, and I can't say why.

## Skipping School on Long Island

When I was six, my family moved to Long Island, not far from New York City. I had more freedom and spent countless hours in a wooded area near our home, just walking around and, of course, talking with the animals.

I could *feel* their emotions—in my heart and in my cells. I loved how animals expressed their dogness, catness, frogness, fishness, lizardness—their beingness. That's empathy, and it seemed natural to me. I feel like I decided to become a field ethologist on the streets of Brooklyn and in the woods of Long Island.

I'll be honest. I wasn't a very good student, particularly in high school. I lettered in three sports and rarely studied. I simply did not want to be sitting at a desk. I used to cut school to hike in the woods. With animals, there was, and is, *always* something to learn.

Occasionally, I broke rules out of compassion for animals. I refused to dissect earthworms or pith frogs in class. That simply felt wrong. I could feel their pain and suffering, just like I could feel the joy and emotions of animals in the woods.

I attribute my compassion for nonhuman animals to my mother's warm, compassionate, and empathic soul, and I attribute my positive thinking to my optimistic father. In retrospect, I know I was extremely lucky to be born into a home where playfulness and laughter were highly valued, as was hard work.

## Birth of an Ethologist and an Activist

Marc studying coyotes on Blacktail Butte, Grand Teton National Park, July 1978.

After getting a bachelor's degree in anthropology, I got a master's in biology and entered an MD/PhD program.

One afternoon during a physiology course, the professor strutted into class sporting a wide grin while carrying a live rabbit. He calmly announced that he was going to kill the rabbit using a "rabbit punch," and we'd use the dead animal in a later experiment. In front of the class, he broke the rabbit's neck by chopping him with the side of his hand. I was astonished and sickened by the spectacle. I refused to participate in the experiment and decided right then to find a different graduate program.

I knew there must be ways of doing science that incorporated respect for animals and allowed people to follow their ethical values. Every time I expressed to people that it was wrong to harm animals for human ends, they would get upset and say, "Oh, you're being anthropomorphic." At the time, most scientists didn't think animals had feelings, so saying they did meant you must be projecting human emotions onto them. I never believed that. I always knew animals had rich inner lives, and I never worried how they compared to ours.

Then I learned about ethologist and veterinarian Michael W. Fox at Washington University. He was way ahead of everybody in terms of animal ethics, and he agreed to be my mentor in their graduate program. Michael was working on the social behavior of dogs, wolves, coyotes, and various canid hybrids (like coydogs), so my early work was on the development of canid behavior. Young animals play a lot, so I studied play, and that interest in the nitty-gritty aspects of animal play has continued for more than five decades.

What I really wanted to do was fieldwork. That led to developing what turned into an eight-and-a-half-year study of wild coyotes in Grand Teton National Park, and for one season I went to Cape Crozier, a remote spot on Ross Island, Antarctica, to study Adélie penguins. From then on, my career was pretty much a straight journey involving fieldwork.

When I became a professor at the University of Colorado, Boulder, the first thing I did was start a no-dissection biology laboratory with an eager graduate student. The department chair didn't think anyone would take it, but in fact, it became the most popular lab in the department.

When I met Jane Goodall in the 1990s, it was a dream come true. We connected deeply about our commitment to animal protection and animal well-being. I began working with Jane's Roots & Shoots group, and in 2002, we cofounded Ethologists for the Ethical Treatment of Animals and cowrote *The Ten Trusts*. We supported each other's work from then on.

Looking back, I credit my parents with allowing me to follow my dreams and my heart. I encourage you to do the same. Snatch every chance you can to follow your heart. One of my father's favorite sayings was, "When opportunity knocks, get off your butt and answer the door."

Marc and Jane toasting during the great crane migration, Nebraska, March 2012.
Photo courtesy of Thomas D. Mangelsen, Images of Nature.

# 1

# good day, sunshine

## Joy, Delight, and Playfulness

One zebra greets another by nipping, Etosha National Park, Namibia. This greeting behavior evolved from grooming behavior, where one zebra would nip down the neck of another. Photo courtesy of Caitlin O'Connell.

This chapter is about happiness, joy, playfulness, pleasure, satisfaction, and humor. The delight of being alive is surely shared by all creatures, even if every animal's experience is unique to them. We may never know the particular joy of bobcats, dolphins, elephants, and ravens, but we recognize joy when we see it.

Whenever you get the chance to observe wild animals playing, that's an encounter worth stopping for—since joy is contagious. While writing this book, Marc had one such encounter while cycling near his Colorado home. He says:

> I came around a corner and right in front of me were three bobcat kittens around four months old—chasing one another, wrestling, doing play bows, and occasionally growling during their rough-and-tumble play. The youngsters paid me no attention as I watched mesmerized. They didn't do anything I haven't seen dogs and wild wolves, coyotes, and foxes do during my many years of play research, but it is a rare treat.
>
> Behind me, a truck slammed to a stop and the driver jumped out. "What's going on—are they fighting?" he asked.
>
> "No," I said, "they're play-fighting."
>
> "Then why are they growling?"
>
> I smiled and said, "You really don't want me to talk about play unless you've got a few hours."
>
> But I did explain, and the driver was intrigued. He couldn't wait to get home and observe his dogs, who often seemed to be fighting. After he left, I stayed a few minutes longer, then I heard what sounded like a larger cat coming through the bushes. In a flash, the pups took off, running toward their mom.
>
> This sort of thing happens all the time with my cycling teammates. We've come across prairie dogs, birds, pigs, and many others. We once watched a group of goats playing "king of the hay bale," and someone remarked, "Wow, they really do that?" Sure, they do!

## Field Notes: Paidia Plays with Her Cubs

For over thirty years, for two months beginning in July, elephant expert Caitlin O'Connell has lived in her research camp at the Mushara waterhole in Namibia's Etosha National Park. The observation tower where the team lives is visible above the tree line. Its three platforms hold tents, supplies, cook stoves, and workstations. Upon arriving every year, their first job is to restraighten the tower. When camp is empty, the elephants like to use the tower's metal frame as a scratching post, causing it to lean.

Every day, animals arrive at the waterhole in shifts like some procession out of *The Lion King*: giraffes, oryx, springboks, zebras, black rhinos, wildebeest, hyenas, and of course, elephants.

As Caitlin describes, Mushara's early visitors sometimes make too much noise for her to sleep:

In Etosha National Park, Nambia, two of Paidia's cubs play. One is trying to tackle the other and is prevented by the expectant paw of his littermate.
Photo courtesy of Caitlin O'Connell.

I awoke in the crisp red dawn of a Namibian desert winter to a soft thudding of footfalls in the sand below. I could hear the faintest murmurings coming from the far edge of the clearing. I sat up in my tent, which was on the top floor of our metal research tower and twenty feet above the waterhole….

Sounds travel well in the still air of early morning. I heard more padding footsteps and a hard thump—followed by even more thudding and what sounded like a full-on chase, tackle, snarl, and romp. The soft calls got closer, short moans, almost a cooing sound. As I became fully awake, I realized these noises could only mean one thing at Mushara—that the resident lioness, Paidia, and her cubs were back at the waterhole and engaged in a rigorous play bout, frisky as ever.

As quietly as I could, I rolled over in my sleeping bag to grab the binoculars.

The early-morning light revealed Paidia and her five yearling cubs lounging against a concrete pillbox bunker where the researchers hide to take close-up photos. Two cubs were making themselves a nest in piles of elephant dung. Then a sibling stalked across the top of the bunker and, tail swishing ominously, jumped, catching them unaware.

Elephant dung and sand flew as a chase ensued. In a burst of feline energy, the tackled sibling quickly got to his feet and ran after his attacker. When he got close enough, the pursuing cub reached a paw out and snagged the hind leg of his prized catch, causing him to tumble. The two cubs rolled around together, taking turns pinning the other down and giving each other huge play bites to the head and throat.

The play bout led to further antics, body contortions, swatting, tail-catching, tripping, and pileups. The other cubs joined in the fun, including mom, who instigated several more play bouts before suddenly running into the shallow pan. There, Paidia stood with all four legs submerged in the ice-cold water, as if inviting the cubs to join her for a dip.

As soon as the friskiest one approached, Paidia immediately charged with claws extended and teeth bared. She ran him out of the water with a smack on the rump as the others looked on from a safe distance, tails perked straight out with surprise and curiosity.

Again, Paidia stood and waited, and again, the same cub took the bait and received the same reprimand. This time, the charge was even more intense, leaving the risk-taker muddy and confused.

Paidia was no longer playing. She was using play to teach her cubs survival skills.

Caitlin O'Connell studying elephants in Etosha National Park, Namibia. Photo courtesy of Tim Rodwell.

Although lions will cross a river if they need to—and I've seen many follow their prey into a shallow pan or even a river—they're not the swimmers that tigers are and often avoid water. It appeared that mom's play bout had turned into a lesson about the perils of water. Considering how close we were to the park border, Paidia could also have been imparting a lesson to her cubs about dangerous boundaries in general....

Over the past fifteen years, I have watched the lioness Bobtail, Paidia's mother, encourage play as part of her family's development. Now Paidia was doing the same for her cubs. That morning, she was using play to hone their instincts of

> self-protection, even as the cubs were learning their own lessons while playing together.

As Marc discovered in his studies of dogs, play is never *just* play. With one another, the lion cubs were practicing their hunting skills: sneaking quietly, tripping and pouncing, biting the throat. "Play might seem like a distraction," Caitlin says, but it is a safe place to learn. "It allows one to experiment with any number of variables, including the element of surprise, without the potential consequences of the real world."

—

## Dogs Just Wanna Have Fun

*In this entry, Marc explains how and why dogs play:*

I've been nose deep in dog play for more than fifty years, and I never get bored. Dogs just wanna have fun, and why not? It's fun watching them play. These are some of *my* field notes from watching three dogs at play—Jethro, a large German shepherd/rottweiler/hound mutt; Zeke, a black lab; and Suki, a Belgian sheepdog:

> Jethro runs toward Zeke, stops immediately in front of him, crouches on his forelimbs, wags his tail, barks, and immediately lunges, biting Zeke's scruff and shaking his head rapidly from side to side. Jethro works his way around to his backside and mounts him, jumps off, does a rapid bow, lunges at his side and slams him with his hips, leaps up and bites his neck, and runs away. Zeke takes off in wild pursuit of Jethro, leaps on his back and bites his muzzle and scruff, then shakes his head rapidly from side to side.
>
> Suki bounds in and chases Jethro and Zeke, and they all wrestle with one another. They part for a few minutes, sniffing here and there and resting. Then

> Jethro walks over to Zeke, extends his paw toward Zeke's head, and nips at his ears. Zeke gets up and jumps on Jethro's back, bites him, and grasps him around his waist. They then fall to the ground and mouth wrestle. They chase and then roll over and play. Suki decides to jump in, and all three frolic until they're exhausted.

For an ethologist, play is a behavior to take seriously. Yet when I first started studying play, a number of my colleagues didn't think so. They thought it was frivolous, even unscientific. At the time, there were very few studies of play, which was considered a wastebasket into which you could throw any behavior you didn't understand.

But evolution is funny. It tends to make critical behaviors—like mating and caring for young—enjoyable, so we'll do them. Since play is defined by joy, it's valid to ask: Why did play evolve? How do we define and recognize it? And how does it help animals survive?

After decades of studying play, I've learned that play is very important, and my research has led to a series of surprising questions:

How do animals communicate that they're playing and not doing something else, like fighting or mating? How do animals play? Does play require certain agreements to ensure cooperation, trust, and reciprocity, as well as to repair trust—such as apologizing—if something goes wrong? If so, does that mean animals have a basic sense of justice or morality?

And if that's true, then is morality an evolved trait? Does "being fair" mean being more fit in evolutionary terms? In other words, do nice guys, gals, and their genes last longest? Do the friendliest and nicest individuals survive best?

That's a lot to get out of watching animals goof off and zoom around. But that's what can happen when you observe animals closely and think carefully about what they do and why.

A black labrador doing a play bow.
Photo by w-ings/iStock.com.

### *Play Starts with a Bow*

Diverse species engage in all types of play, including playing with objects or going crazy with "zoomies"—when animals madly run all over the place as if they've lost their minds. I've seen coyotes, wolves, red foxes, black bears, elk, penguins, and many others get silly.

For a model of fair play, let's go to the dogs. Dogs signal social play using the "play bow." This is what Jethro does first in my field notes above: He crouches on his forelegs, his hindlegs straight and his tail wagging. With or without barking, this is how dogs say, *I wanna play with you!*

Many species have their own versions of the play bow, and animals use other play signals—such as faking left and going right or approaching someone and then running away to get them to chase. With dogs, the play bow both initiates play and keeps it going if there's a break. It's used whenever something happens that might end play. For instance, if a dog is about to do something, or just did something, that might be misinterpreted—like growling viciously and biting—the play bow says, *I'm going to bite you, but it's only in play.* Or: *I didn't mean to bite so hard, let's keep playing.*

So, if you don't want to play, don't bow.

Two other important play behaviors are role-reversing and self-handicapping (also called "play inhibition"). These equalize differences in size or dominance rank between players to create a "level playing field." This promotes the give-and-take and cooperation that's needed for play to occur.

For example, if a large dominant dog is playing with a much smaller dog, the large dog won't bite as hard or play as vigorously as they can. They might roll over on their back so the small dog can attack them, which they'd never allow in a real fight. This is obvious when different-size dogs play tug-of-war with a rope: The stronger dog could pull hard and "win" every time, but they don't. The goal is to play together, not to dominate. I once observed a larger dog accidentally pull the rope so hard the other dog lifted off the ground—and the first dog immediately dropped the rope, ran over to the smaller dog, and play bowed. In essence, the bow was an "apology" to ask if they could keep playing.

There are more play signals. Dogs invite play by creeping forward on their stomach, tail wagging. They sometimes engage in play pants (or rapid breathing). Some species even have play scents. Research has found that a species of voles emits a pheromone from the back of their heads that stimulates play in other voles. Dogs and other animals might have the same thing, but we don't know yet.

The contagious joy of play is perhaps the most recognizable sign. Still, it's important to remember that identifying emotions is much easier than understanding the how and why of animal behavior. To correctly interpret the complex interactions and social behaviors involved in an expression of joy requires training, experience, and research.

### *What Is Play and Why Is It Important?*

On the surface, play serves no obvious purpose. Play is improvisational and mixes a hodgepodge of behaviors from other contexts, like fighting, mating, hunting, self-defense, and so on. Dogs might growl, bite, hump, and chase in quick succession, and they might exaggerate, minimize, and interrupt these behaviors. After growling fiercely, they might bite softly, and after mounting and starting to hump, they might abruptly quit and take turns chasing. That kaleidoscope of behaviors helps identify play.

Since play goes by in a blur, one way my students and I have studied play is to analyze videos. We record a play session and review it frame by frame, so we can track the dynamics. It's essential to pay attention to subtle details that can be lost or go unnoticed when, for instance, we are simply watching dogs in the park. Dogs and other animals keep close track of every move, so we need to keep track, too. Yep, analyzing videos frame by frame is tedious, and some students have had second thoughts about studying play after doing this!

Yet it's through such meticulous study that we've learned why play is important. Play fosters physical development and motor skills, it provides critical socialization, it helps develop physical life skills (like hunting and self-defense), and it develops the mind, in part by allowing animals to train for unexpected situations. That kaleidoscope of behaviors serves a purpose. Play feeds brain, body, and community—teaching young animals what they will need to do to survive in the world as well as the interpersonal skills to thrive in their own society.

Social play is almost like school for nonhuman animals, and because it's fun, no animal ever skips class.

I think the most important benefits are social. Play helps individuals within the group to get along, since play relies on and teaches trust, cooperation, niceness, fairness, forgiveness, and humility. Through play, immature individuals learn the ground rules of acceptable behavior and how to resolve conflicts in a situation that is safe, enjoyable, and nonthreatening, where the stakes and consequences are low. Kids are encouraged to play organized sports for the same reasons.

### *The Golden Rules of Play: Fairness Matters*

Uncooperative play is an oxymoron. When cooperation and fairness break down, play not only stops, it becomes virtually impossible to enjoy.

Research shows that, among humans, cooperating and being fair feels good. This may be another reason animals love to play. And all of this might help explain how morality evolved.

Across many different species, there's little evidence that play signals are used to deceive others. Play signals are honest signals; only very rarely are they used to hide aggressive intentions. Animals almost never say, *I want to play with you*, and then, when the other animal is vulnerable, engage in a real attack.

Most likely, this is because there are sanctions for lying. Individuals who don't play fair become increasingly isolated—they are avoided as playmates. In extreme cases, they can be shunned from the group. I often say, animals who play together stay together. Research shows this to be generally true for social carnivores and other animals. That's one vital way play improves survival

In essence, animal play appears to rely on the universal human value of the Golden Rule: Do unto others as you would have them do unto you. I summarize this as "the four golden rules of play":

1. Ask first and communicate clearly: This is the function of the play bow and other play signals, to reiterate the intention to play.
2. Mind your manners: This is the function of self-handicapping and role-reversing, to not take advantage.
3. Admit when you are wrong: The play bow can function as an apology, and forgiveness is almost always offered. Animals usually continue playing after a mistake.
4. Be honest: If animals aren't sincerely trying to play in a safe, fair way, then play ends.

Social play is thus based on a foundation of fairness that is perhaps a uniquely egalitarian behavior. Animals exhibit fairness during play, and they react negatively to unfair behavior. If we define morality as a set of social rules and expectations that neutralize differences among individuals in an effort to maintain group harmony, then that's exactly what we find in animals when they play.

That isn't the same as human morality or ethics. For one thing, fairness during play is about an individual's specific social expectations and not some universally defined standard of right and wrong.

Rather, research shows that a moral sensibility is a wide-ranging biological necessity for social living, and that morality may be a broadly adaptive strategy that has evolved in many species. I call this type of moral behavior "wild justice."

In other words, just as emotions are a gift of our ancestors—something that evolution has passed down to most if not all creatures—so too are the basic ingredients of morality, namely: cooperation, empathy, fairness, justice, and trust.

That's an amazing thing to uncover by studying play.

—

## Wildlife Guide: Animals at Play

Like the truck driver watching the bobcat cubs, we sometimes have a hard time identifying whether animals are fighting or playing.

This wildlife guide shows what play looks like in a handful of species. Joy is usually the first clue, but pay attention to all behaviors: Are bodies loose and relaxed? Do animals take turns, switch places, and reverse roles? Are there ritualized signals resembling play bows?

"Joy jumps" are another common play signal. Ethologist Frans de Waal said, "The joy jump is so recognizable that it is easily understood between species. In captivity, a rhino calf may play with a dog, or a dog with an otter, or a foal with a goat, and in the wild young chimpanzees have been observed wrestling with baboons, and ravens and wolves teasing each other."

As de Waal said, "Play has its own universal language."

Whenever you see animals interacting energetically, observe from a distance and ask, "Fighting or playing?" What do *you* think?

### *Zebras*

At the Mushara waterhole in Namibia's Etosha National Park, Caitlin O'Connell has found that the greetings of zebra stallions are like extended bro hugs.

The male leaders "form little greeting parties," she says. "The harem stallions nuzzle, wrap necks, nip, and sniff one another around the head and sometimes the genitals. Then they exhibit an exaggerated chewing behavior with their teeth bared and the corners of their lips drawn up as if smiling or laughing with necks extended and ears directed forward. It really looks like they are enjoying a hilarious joke together."

Then everyone defecates to form "a communal dung pile."

Hmph. Males obsessing over poop. Sound familiar?

Meanwhile, younger stallions, heads bobbing, also greet with playful, harmless nips to the neck that are invitations to chase. Some threaten kicks and try to knock others over, and O'Connell says, "this dynamic can escalate into more aggressive play, including raising up on hind legs and kicking at each other with front legs while attempting to bite the other's neck."

None of it is serious. Macho posturing and joking threats are just how male zebras diffuse tension and build trust.

Nothing recognizable there, either.

### *Elephants*

When she first joined the Amboseli Elephant Research Project in Kenya, scientist Vicky Fishlock was confused by some elephant behavior. She was told the elephants were "being silly."

"I thought, *Silly?*" Fishlock says. "The next thing I know, a full-grown female comes along walking on her knees and throwing her head around, acting just daffy. They were just happy. They were like, 'Yaay!' Everyone says how smart they are. But they can be ridiculous, too.... I actually had one male kneel down right in front of the car and throw zebra bones at me, trying to get me to play with him.... Sometimes they put bushes on their heads and just look at you like that—ridiculous."

Elephant calves play in Amboseli National Park, Kenya, 2012.
Photo courtesy of Thomas D. Mangelsen, Images of Nature.

Fishlock says it's easy to tell they're playing by their "floppy" demeanor. Any expressions of fear or seriousness are exaggerated "for the humor value," as if "they're all in on the game."

Fishlock finds that males tend to play "pushing contests against each other," while "females tend to play 'I'm chasing enemies.'"

Caitlin O'Connell likens the sparring of male elephants to arm wrestling, martial arts, or jousting. While, she says, "in very young calves, the invitation to play is more of a pig pile or a mud-bath tackle—no formal invitation necessary."

### *Giraffes*

For giraffes, the signature play behavior is called necking. O'Connell describes this as "wrapping their necks around one another and then slamming their horn-like ossicones into the flank of the other."

This is partly sparring practice, but O'Connell says this also "teaches them an important courtship ritual, where the slow and intimate wrapping of necks is a determinant of mating success."

### *Rats*

As a student, neuroscientist Jaak Panksepp had a pet rat named Tulip who loved to play toss—with herself.

"Whenever I returned home," Panksepp said, "she was especially eager for a little game wherein I'd toss her gently from one end of a couch to the other. She'd eagerly scurry back for more and more of this fun. I usually tired of it long before she did."

Later, Panksepp studied play in rats and found they have a "deep desire" for "rough-and-tumble play" and love to be tickled at the nape of the neck. "Rats even chirp with joy when they're playing," he said. "When we started to listen carefully to the sounds they made during play—sounds inaudible to us without special equipment—the air was filled with short, high-frequency vocalizations."

Is this rat laughter? Panksepp thought this chirping might be. This highlights one reason why it can be hard for us to recognize animal emotions: Other animals can express themselves in ways we humans can't hear, smell, taste, or see.

But it wasn't hard to tell the rats were enjoying themselves.

"When we tickled them, the rats also tried to reciprocate—to play with us. They gently nipped our fingers, especially if we paused in our play, apparently in an attempt to solicit more. I've been 'bitten' thousands of times by young rats, but never seriously. Just like puppies or kittens, they never break the skin in their playful eagerness."

### *Macaws, Parrots, Crows, and Ravens*

Currently, only a few bird species are known to play. Those who do are mostly parrots and corvids—particularly macaws, keas, African grey parrots, crows, and ravens. Yet the chipper tomfoolery of these avians rivals that of dolphins.

Macaws in the wild are waggish clowns. When friends meet, they typically "start fooling around, hanging upside down, billing, and gently biting," says ecologist Carl Safina. During flock-wide congregations at clay licks, macaws will drop pieces of clay on birds below, while caged macaws are infamous for dropping objects onto others as well as pooping on four-legged pets.

The large, New Zealand parrots known as keas are, science writer Jennifer Ackerman claims, "the king of fowl play." New Zealanders call them "mountain monkeys." Ackerman says that keas "go around in juvenile gangs trashing things, deconstructing windshield wipers and the vinyl trim on cars, as well as campers' tents and backpacks, rain gutters, and outdoor furniture.... The birds have been known to steal television antennae from houses and deflate automobile tires. One kea was observed rolling up a doormat and pushing it down a flight of steps."

Apparently, crows and ravens love playing in snow. In the mountains outside Hokkaido, Japan, a pair of ravens were seen frolicking in fresh powder. One lay on their breast to slide down the slope while the other rolled, legs in the air; once at the bottom, they flew to the top to do it again. Crows have been videoed skidding down a children's slide and "snowboarding" on a snow-covered roof by riding a plastic disc.

### *Bees*

Do busy bees ever stop to play ball? Turns out, sometimes they will.

Recent research has shown that bumble bees, particularly adolescent bees, will voluntarily roll wooden balls with no instruction and for no purpose or reward, and they will choose to do this over and over again, even when they know that food is waiting elsewhere.

"It is certainly mind-blowing, at times amusing," said Samadi Galpayage, one of the study's authors, "to watch bumble bees show something like play.... It goes to show, once more, that despite their little size and tiny brains, they are more than small robotic beings."

Indeed, a study published in October 2025 showed that bumble bees feel and share joy. Given a sugar treat, they perk up, explore more, and become more adventurous. Further, when other bees see a happy bee, they become happier, too. Sharing feelings is called "emotional contagion," which is something all social animals possess but had never been seen before in social insects.

Perhaps everyone likes a good time.

## What Are Emotions?

It's a simple question that's surprisingly tricky to answer: What are emotions?

To study animal emotions, we need to define them, but scientists struggle to agree on a single definition. Emotions can arise consciously and unconsciously. Some are instinctual or automatic responses to events, and some we choose to feel. Emotions can be reactions to thoughts, physical sensations, and hormones, and they can cause thoughts, physical sensations, and bursts of hormones. Emotions are internal experiences, yet they are different from thoughts or word-based reasoning.

In general, emotions arise from bodily sensations and generate physical or behavioral responses, such as when sights or sounds trigger hormones that prompt a fight-or-flight response. Emotions show themselves by the behaviors they inspire.

Scientists often distinguish emotions from feelings. Most people use these words to mean the same thing (and we use them interchangeably in this book). Yet emotions can be considered "raw data," like the fear that can arise when a shadow makes us duck. Feelings come next and are generated by thoughts; they are responses to our evaluation of a situation, like a story that provides meaning. First, a sensation triggers fear and we duck, but if the shadow turns out to be nothing, we might choose to feel relieved and laugh. If we discover that a friend deliberately tried to scare us, we might get angry and yell at them.

In the broadest terms, emotions are psychological phenomena that help us manage our behavior. They help us decide what to do in the most effective or appropriate way. They prompt us to run when we should run and to relax when there isn't a problem.

Emotions are divided between primary and secondary emotions. Primary emotions are involuntary and don't require conscious thought. Famed biologist Charles Darwin, the founder of evolutionary theory, identified six: fear, anger, disgust, surprise, sadness, and happiness.

Secondary emotions are more complex and not automatic; these thought-based feelings help us choose what to do. Many are also considered "social" emotions, which are feelings related to relationships—like jealousy, guilt, compassion, grief, shame, devotion, embarrassment, and so on.

At one time, the majority of scientists believed few nonhuman animals experienced any emotions. Most animals were considered more like robots who behaved according to preprogrammed instinct, not choice. Over the last two decades, scientific opinion has reversed. Due to a wide variety of research—including brain scans and studies of the neurochemical bases of emotion—we know that most animals are capable of feeling and that their feelings influence their behavior. The ongoing breakthroughs in ethology are challenging many of our long-held assumptions about the supposed inferiority or limits of animal minds.

That said, it's very important to emphasize that just because many different species express similar emotions, that doesn't mean all species feel or think the same way. They probably don't. Each species has its own experience, unique to their particular senses and society: There is elephant joy, pig fear, dolphin anger, parrot pleasure, penguin envy, chimpanzee grief, octopus curiosity, and on and on.

Further, individuals differ, too. They have their own experiences and personalities and feelings, which can differ from other individuals of their species.

Emotions may be universal, but each individual, and each species, is their own nation.

## Jokers of the Sea

Dolphins seem to wring as much joy out of life as possible. They are self-aware, curiosity-driven, emotionally intelligent pranksters. The cool kids everyone wants to hang with.

Two bottlenose dolphins leap out of the ocean.
Photo copyright © 2025 maddalenabearzi/OCS (under NOAA permit).

### *Bubble Rings, Feathers, and Hula Hoops*

To perform for the public, captive dolphins and killer whales—who are not whales but the largest species of dolphin—are trained using fish rewards. They do tricks primarily to get fed, but that doesn't mean they don't also enjoy performing. Cetaceans *love* to play—anytime, anywhere, with anyone.

They particularly love playing when they're "off the clock."

Captive dolphins teach themselves—through practice and by observing other dolphins—how to exhale from their blowhole to create bubble rings, the same way we blow smoke rings. This takes skill. Dolphins aren't born knowing this technique. Once they get it right, they experiment every which way.

Dolphin researcher Diana Reiss has studied bubble play in awe. She's watched groups of dolphins drop pieces of fish from above to see how they interact with bubble rings. In shallow pools, she says, "the dolphins turn to one side and blow rings horizontally. Then they spin the rings like kids with hoops, using deft flicks of their rostrums [snouts] to spin the rings without touching them."

Dolphins learn to flip rings 180 degrees, merge two rings into one, and create "water snakes, undulating silver streams of air that they chase," Reiss says. Air bubbles rise, but dolphins learn to keep them near the bottom of pools by making them smaller—knocking a segment out of a ring and splicing the main ring back together with a twitch.

Bubble play demonstrates "active minds at work," Reiss says. Not to mention a sense of aesthetics. Like a snooty critic, a dolphin displeased with a particular ring will bite it to disperse it and try again.

Dolphins play with any objects they can reach, tossing balls, toys, plastic bags, frisbees, you name it. Researcher Maddalena Bearzi watched five wild dolphins play keep-away with kelp like "a group of kids playing football in a city playground." A pair of captive dolphins once invented a game where they towed each other with a hula hoop. Ecologist Carl Safina describes killer whales who "amuse themselves with a feather, balancing it on their nose, then letting it go and catching it with a fin, then letting it go and catching it with a fluke [tail]."

Most famously, wild dolphins ride the bow waves of boats, they surf shore waves, and they engage in unprompted acrobatics, breaching, leaping, and jumping out of sheer pleasure. As Bearzi writes, "Joy seems to be contagious among dolphins."

### *Punks and Practical Jokers*

Dolphins and killer whales are not above juvenile pranks, either. They will punk other creatures for no good reason than their own amusement.

Wild dolphins, Bearzi says, "may toss a fish in the air with their beak and then grab it again and again as if in a silly mood.... They may tease a sea turtle by pulling on its tail or imitate the movement of a small shark by swimming in a side-to-side motion."

Captive killer whales sometimes wait till people are gathered by their tank and then splash them with their tails.

Diana Reiss herself was the victim of a practical joke during a feeding session with Delphi, a dolphin in her research program. She was feeding Delphi fish one by one, and each time, he gave an "exaggerated swallow," which Reiss had never seen before.

He wasn't really swallowing. "Delphi's eyes got really big," Reiss says, "the way they do when the dolphins are excited. Delphi opened his mouth, and I saw all these whole fish in there. He must have been holding them in his throat or had regurgitated them."

Then Delphi shook his head, spraying fish everywhere, including all over Reiss.

"I laughed hysterically," Reiss says. "I couldn't help myself. Delphi had completely fooled me, completely manipulated me. And from what I could tell from his demeanor, he seemed to know it."

Not everyone is amused by dolphin mischief.

Marine biologist Bernd Würsig says that the dangling skinny legs and webbed feet of floating seabirds are, perhaps, irresistible:

> I've often seen a lone dusky dolphin approach such a pair of appendages, generally belonging to a kelp gull, slow its speed to almost nothing, open its tooth-lined jaws gingerly (so as not to disturb the oblivious bird above), and gently but firmly close its jaws around one or both legs. Then, surging forward with a sideways toss of the torso, the dolphin pulls the hapless avian beneath the waves. The surprised bird flutters and kicks, the dolphin releases its grip, and the bird bobs to the surface for a frenzy of preening before it flaps off. It's unhurt, save perhaps for its pride.

## What Is Ethology?

*Ethology* is the study of animal behavior. It focuses mainly on wild animals in their natural habitats, although some ethological work has involved captive animals. *Cognitive ethology* refers specifically to the study of animal minds—what's in them and how they work, their thoughts and feelings.

In 1973, ethologists Konrad Lorenz, Niko Tinbergen, and Karl von Frisch shared the Nobel Prize in Physiology and Medicine for their discoveries related to animal behavior. Today, the field of compassionate conservation relies on research in this ever-growing discipline.

Cognitive ethologists want to know what it is like to be another animal. What is *their* lived experience from *their* point of view? What do they see, hear, and smell? Why do they do what they do? Some empirical scientific evidence combined with common sense and intuition is all it takes to get a pretty reliable picture of who animals are and what they want and need.

Ethologists are also interested in other important questions: How and why have emotions and behaviors evolved among living beings? How do animals adapt their behaviors to succeed in a changing situation or environment, and/or how do changing environments cause animals to adapt? How do behaviors develop within an individual or society?

Flexibility of behavior—that is, the ability to change your response when things around you change—is a sign of awareness, or what scientists call a mark of consciousness. This shows that an animal is thinking and acting with intention, not instinct. The animal is evaluating their situation, considering past experiences, and deciding what to do based on the present moment and imagined future interactions.

Studying the evolution of emotions and behavior is important. Like physical genes, individuals inherit mental capacities and behaviors, and as the behavior of individuals change, species also can change. Humans are not the only animals who think and feel, and the theory of evolution holds that whatever attributes we possess must, in some form, have also been present in our ancestors and still be present in related species. As Darwin proposed, in many cases the distinctions among species are differences of degree, not kind.

We sometimes forget that we, too, are animals. Further, what animals share in terms of emotions far outweighs the differences, which can be minor.

As famous primatologist Frans de Waal once said: "We like to see ourselves as special, but whatever the difference between humans and animals may be, it is unlikely to be found in the emotional domain."

## Get Started: Anyone Can Do Citizen Science

In practice, all scientific research comes down to the same thing—asking good, specific questions and conducting close, detailed observations. Citizen science is when people who aren't formally trained as scientists conduct their own research or help gather information for studies run by others. We hope this book inspires readers to observe animals more closely and so join humanity's ongoing effort to understand what makes animals tic.

"I think it's a lot of fun to watch and study animals," Marc says, "and you don't need to be a trained scientist to do it. All you need is curiosity."

For example, when Jane Goodall first went to Tanzania to study chimpanzees, she didn't yet have university training. "Although it was the sort of thing I most wanted to do," Jane once said, "I was not qualified to undertake a scientific study of animal behavior." But Louis Leakey, the paleontologist who sent her, "wanted someone with a mind uncluttered and unbiased by theory who would make the study for no other reason than a real desire for knowledge. And, in addition, someone with a sympathetic understanding of animals."

Marc meets people like this all the time, such as in dog parks. People are often surprised to discover how much we still don't know about animals and can learn by observing them in our daily lives. Citizen science helps uncover new information and raise unasked questions that inspire formal research.

Marc gets contacted all the time by students asking for help with school-related research projects on animal behavior and emotions; this is citizen science. He helps when he can, and here are a couple of examples:

1. As an eighth grader, Alexandra contacted Marc to ask if he knew whether familiar dogs play differently than unfamiliar dogs. She thought this was a silly question, but Marc assured her this hadn't been studied before. Alexandra developed an ethogram (see below) of dog play behaviors based on Marc's previous research, and she observed her own dogs in a dog park. Her fieldwork became a family affair, with her sister and parents as assistants. Alexandra's research won a science fair award and, Marc says, "if she'd had more time to pursue it, it could have been a published paper in a professional journal."
2. Two middle-school friends, Milo and Maya, once convinced their school to allow them to set up trail cameras on their school grounds so they could study the behavior of urban gray foxes as part of an ethology club they founded. The project was inspired by the research of Bill Leikam, "the Fox Guy."
3. Sixth-grader Sheldon wanted to study color preferences in mice. Sheldon's father helped build the outdoor enclosure where he did his research. While Sheldon's prediction turned out to be true—that mice prefer green—he discovered it was for an unexpected reason (related to how mice perceive color) that expanded his knowledge of rodents.

Occasionally, citizen science inspires people to become scientists. Marc was recently contacted by Gunnar Tribelhorn, who had noticed what seemed like play behavior among the fish in his fish tank. After conducting his own study and publishing the results, Gunnar changed careers to become an ethologist.

If you want to try it yourself, here is Marc's short seven-step guide:

*Step 1: Ask a specific question related to emotions, intelligence, or social behavior.*

For example, years ago, I wanted to learn about self-awareness in dogs. My question was: Can dogs recognize themselves and/or distinguish themselves from other dogs?

*Step 2: Rephrase the question in a way that can be quantified using observable behaviors.*

Self-awareness is very hard to show with any species because animals experience the world so much differently than we do. Since smell is the primary sense for dogs, I devised a simple sniff test using my own dog, Jethro. I asked: Could Jethro tell his urine from that of other dogs? Many dog owners know dogs can, but this had never been shown in an experiment.

*Step 3: Develop a method for testing the observed behaviors.*

This might have been the hardest part. Dogs sniff first and ask questions later—and that includes pee and each other's butts. So how could I get Jethro to sniff in a way that indicated he was recognizing his own pee—and by extension himself? I developed the "yellow snow test." During winter, I picked up urine-saturated yellow snow created by Jethro and other dogs and moved it to different places along a path. I did this without Jethro seeing me, and I used rubber gloves, which I changed each time to avoid mixing odors. Then I walked with Jethro and recorded his reactions.

*Step 4: Create measurable criteria of the observed behaviors.*

I measured three main things: whether Jethro sniffed pee, how long he sniffed, and whether he peed or "marked over" the pee. We know that dogs engage in territorial "scent wars" by peeing over the urine of other dogs, and males do this more often with other males.

*Step 5: Collect and track your data.*

There are many methods for collecting and tracking data. The backbone of all ethological research is an ethogram, which lists the actions that animals perform. An ethogram is like a menu of behaviors that describes what the animal does, but without explaining why they did it. With dogs, a few examples might be bowing, pawing, muzzle bite, tail position, howling, and so on. The number of actions you decide to record might increase or decrease as research continues and you refine your observations.

To track behaviors, you can write them down or speak into a voice recorder. You can also film behaviors and review them frame by frame. You might record all observed behaviors over a set amount of time, record only specific behaviors (like the yellow snow test), or combine approaches. You might look for behavior patterns in only one context or in many contexts. The best approach depends on the questions you're asking and what you're looking for.

*Step 6: Gather enough data to be statistically significant.*

I didn't do the yellow snow test once. I did it regularly over five winters when there was enough snow on the ground. People who saw me moving yellow snow would ask what I was doing and shake their heads in disbelief—*crazy scientists!* However, it's easy to jump to wrong conclusions with a small sample size. To avoid this, it's important to repeat tests and confirm similar results many times. If results differ a lot, there might be a problem with the test, the criteria, the conditions, or the original question.

*Step 7: Summarize and publicize your conclusions.*

Analyze your data, write them up, and share or publish what you learned! Write a school report or blog post, or send it to a magazine, newspaper, or even a professional journal.

Ultimately, Jethro spent more time sniffing and marking the urine of others, and he marked over the urine of males more than females. Thus, Jethro clearly knew which pee was his, and my research gave rise to more controlled studies. While this doesn't show that dogs have a sense of self like we do—a sense of "I-ness," perhaps—they do recognize themselves. Dogs have a sense of "me-ness" and "you-ness."

# 2

# lean on me

## Empathy and Compassion

A baby chimpanzee clings to their mother, Gombe National Park, Tanzania.
Photo courtesy of Thomas D. Mangelsen, Images of Nature.

Many animals possess empathy, or the ability to recognize and relate to another being's feelings. Compassion means caring about someone else's feelings. Whenever we help someone feel better—knowing that we'll be unhappy if they are unhappy—we are expressing empathy and compassion.

Empathy happens naturally, but caring is a choice. Just because we know how someone feels doesn't mean we have to do anything about it. So, compassion is often recognized through action: by consoling someone who's sad or in pain or celebrating someone else's achievement.

For instance, retired social work professor Mark Dyke recently shared this story with Marc:

"I have a small pond of koi fish," he wrote. "And one of them jumped out. I found it on the patio beside the pond trying to breathe."

Using a net, Mark returned the koi to the water, but the fish didn't move. He tried over and over to encourage the fish to swim, but nothing worked, and finally, he gave up, letting the koi sink to the bottom. Then something "stunning" happened.

"I noticed several koi and a goldfish swim under the dying koi," he wrote, "and push it up toward the surface. This happened several times, and then the injured koi swam away. I wouldn't have believed this if I hadn't seen it myself."

As this chapter's stories show, recognizing how someone feels is often what inspires caring. That's what helps bond families, friends, and communities. Empathy and compassion are essential for survival. They are two of evolution's most important emotional gifts.

—

## Jethro and Bunny

*Here, Marc shares a story about Jethro, who was his companion dog for twelve years:*

Jethro was a rescue mutt I met at the Boulder Humane Society. He was about nine months old and looked part-Rottweiler, part-German shepherd, with a little bit of hound thrown in. He was black and tan, somewhat barrel-chested, with dripping jowls and long floppy ears. Jethro was low-key, gentle, and well-mannered. Even as a puppy, compassion defined him.

At the humane society, he sought out friendships with other dogs, cats, ducks, geese, and goats, and he never chased animals around my mountain home. He loved to just hang out and watch the world go by.

Marc's dog Jethro and his stuffed bunny.

One day, while I was inside, I heard Jethro come to the front door. Instead of whining to come in like usual, he just sat there. Then I noticed a small furry object in his mouth.

My first reaction was, *Oh no, he killed a bird.*

I opened the door, and Jethro belched a very young bunny at my feet, drenched in his saliva. I couldn't see any injuries, just a small bundle of fur who needed care, warmth, food, and love. Jethro looked up at me, wide-eyed and standing tall, as if he wanted to be praised for being such a good Samaritan. I did so. He was clearly proud of his compassionate self, and he kept looking at me as if to say: *Come on, do something*.

I guessed that the bunny's mother had disappeared. Perhaps she'd been eaten by one of the coyotes, red foxes, black bears, or cougars who also lived near my house.

### *Taking Care of Bunny*

I picked the bunny up and gathered a box, a small piece of cloth for a blanket, and some water, and put her inside. The whole time, Jethro followed me around, whined, and tried to snatch her from my hands.

I named the bunny "Bunny" (very original!) and fed her some mashed-up carrots, celery, and lettuce. Jethro stood behind me, panting, dripping saliva, and watching my every move. I was concerned he would go for Bunny or the food, but he only watched, fascinated by this little ball of fur as she slowly got comfortable in her new home.

I didn't want to leave Jethro alone with Bunny, but he wouldn't move, even when I offered him a treat. All day, he remained steadfast near Bunny until, finally, I had to drag him outside for his nightly walk. When we returned, he beelined for the box, and that's where he slept throughout the night.

I trusted Jethro wouldn't harm Bunny, and he didn't. During the two weeks I nursed her back to health, Jethro adopted Bunny as his friend and made sure no one harmed her.

Finally, the day came when I reintroduced Bunny to the outdoors. Jethro strolled along. As I released her, Jethro and I watched her cautiously make her way into a woodpile to hide. An hour later, Bunny reemerged and boldly hopped off, beginning life as a full-fledged rabbit.

The whole time, Jethro never took his eyes off Bunny. But he didn't try to approach her or snatch her. After she was gone, Jethro sniffed around the woodpile where Bunny had taken temporary refuge—as if expecting his friend to emerge.

For a few months, Bunny hung around, showing no concern at our presence. Yet for six months, long after Bunny had disappeared, every time I let Jethro out, he immediately ran to the woodpile and cocked his head from side-to-side, looking for her. When I called out "Bunny" in a high-pitched voice, Jethro would whine, hoping to see his friend again.

After that, Jethro watched all the bunnies and adult rabbits who came and went near our house, perhaps wondering if they were Bunny. He tried to get as close as he could to them, but he never chased them when they ran away.

### *Saving a Life, Again*

Jethro was a compassionate soul. Nine years after he met Bunny, he once again came running up to me with a wet animal in his mouth.

*Hmm*, I wondered, *another bunny?*

This time the wet ball he dropped at my feet was a young bird who had flown into a window and been stunned. I held the bird in my hands for a few minutes as they regained their senses, and Jethro, true to form, watched my and the bird's every move. When I thought the bird was ready to fly, I placed them on my porch railing. Jethro approached, sniffed, stepped back, and watched the bird fly away.

Jethro saved two animals from death. He could easily have gulped down each one. But you don't do that to friends, do you?

## Childhood Inspiration: Maddalena Bearzi

A lifelong desire to connect with, study, and help animals often starts in childhood. In this book's Childhood Inspiration sidebars, six people share their early experiences with animals and nature and describe how that impacted their lives and sometimes inspired their careers.

Maddalena Bearzi is a marine ecologist and conservationist who's been studying Pacific Ocean marine mammals for over twenty-five years. The president and cofounder of the Ocean Conservation Society, Maddalena was born and raised in Italy.

> I often think of the times, as a little girl, I sat on the deserted shores of Orvile in Sardinia. Every summer, the sea teeming with life would beckon me, day after day. Beneath the surface of salty Mediterranean waters, I might gently tickle the sticky arm of an octopus hiding under a rock or chase after small fish swarming into a bait ball to escape predators. Lobsters were large; groupers, sea bass, flounders, morays, and seabreams were plentiful. I could lose myself in observing the tiny creatures of the intertidal zone or playing with the hair-like strands of *Posidonia*. On land, I wandered freely in the brushwood among flocks of sheep. There were no tourists, noise, or litter; only wildlife as far as my eyes could see. I remember thinking that if paradise existed, it wouldn't be different from this unspoiled haven. Summers ended and I returned to the city; the Mediterranean scent of junipers and myrtles never failed to follow me home.
>
> On those pristine shores, I fell in love with nature; a love strong enough to endure a lifetime. As I grew older, I observed small and large animals in many wild places, both at sea and on land. Over the years, though, I watched as our human arrogance toward Mother Earth grew. Now, I hesitate to return to Orvile, fearful that the paradise of my youth is no more.
>
> My love for nature has become a battle to protect it. Much has been lost, but there is still wilderness to explore, much at stake, and much work to be done.

## Taking Care of the Flock

Chickens have long gotten a bad rap as dumb birds, but research shows that the ignorance is our own.

Chickens can recognize up to a hundred individuals. They invent games and give gifts, like shiny objects to human owners. Their clucks and calls communicate specific information, like the presence of food and particular predators, but they are also devious and deceptive. If a hawk flies overhead, a rooster will raise an alarm if hens are nearby but remain silent if only a rival rooster is exposed. Roosters have even passed the famous "mirror test"—in which an animal who recognizes their reflection in a mirror is considered self-aware.

Sy with one of the flock.
Photo by Vicki Stiefel.

Naturalist Sy Montgomery has shared her property with free-ranging chickens for decades. She says they are "smart, sensitive individuals who can be wonderfully inventive and affectionate companions." Sy told Marc the following story:

> I was taking care of my neighbor's flock—a flock my own last surviving chicken had joined—and a bear tore off the back of my neighbor's coop one night and ate two hens. I had to move the rest of the chickens to *my* coop about a half mile away before the bear could come back and finish everyone off.
>
> After such a traumatizing event, how to make them feel at home in a new coop? I first moved *my* hen and her best friend (next to whom she always roosted each night) … and my hen took up the *exact* perch she used to roost on, with her best friend next to her.

> When I moved the rest of the hens, they felt calm and at home—they were picking up on my hen's comforting memories of this place, which she clearly shared with her best friend and spread to the rest of the flock.
>
> I thought that was pretty extraordinary: not that my hen remembered her old home, and not that her friendship with the other hens was that strong. What was amazing was that it was so easy for a mere human to see this!

Journalist Tove Danovich has also tended her own flock for years and says chickens are "far from interchangeable." Each has their own unique personality with "very different approaches to conflict and conflict management."

She told Marc this story:

> Peggy was one of the first chicks I ever got, and even as more birds were added to the flock, she stayed "head hen" of the bunch. I think of her as a very benevolent ruler. The flock is pretty stable but fights do break out from time to time. Whenever two hens are squabbling, Peggy's first step is always to run over and place her body in between them. Sometimes this is enough to make the fighting hens walk away. Other times, one of the hens will try to get another peck in. That's when Peggy will reach out and jump on top of the bully hen, pecking at her and chasing her away. It has very "you had your warning!" energy.

Peggy is six years old today, and Tove says, "She didn't do this when she was a younger hen. It's something she's picked up over time. It's fascinating to me that Peggy always gives everyone a chance to just cool down and end the fight."

# JOB APPLICATION

**Rat Lifeguard at the Rodent Pool***

| Personal Information | |
|---|---|
| Full Name: Rat (genus Rattus) | |
| Address: Pretty much everywhere people are | |
| Email: N/A | Phone: Just shout |

| Position Information |
|---|
| Position Applied For: Rat Lifeguard |
| Desired Salary: Will work for peanuts, chocolate, cheese, bananas, and berries |
| Date Available to Start: Anytime, today works |

| Educational Background |
|---|
| Lifelong attendance in the school of hard knocks; graduated summa cum laude (have survived several mass extinctions, including the one that knocked off the dinosaurs) |
| Audited human classrooms from grade school through college, mostly as a drop-in student |

| Other Training |
|---|
| Know how to swim but definitely prefer not to, except in emergencies like sinking ships. Don't even like getting wet. But to save a drowning rat, we would. |

| Work History |
|---|
| Most recent jobs include bomb-detection work; humans say we have a nose for it |
| Extensive restaurant experience (see Ratatouille) |
| Way too many jobs in human research labs. Working conditions horrible, even deadly; desire for new employment is reason for current job search. Studies confirm our qualifications as rodent lifeguards (see references). |

* *Authors' Note:* This job application is a joke. There are no rat lifeguards, since rodent pools don't exist. However, research studies that cause pain and distress to animals in order to prove those animals feel and think continue to be conducted. If rats could talk, we believe they'd say: Researchers should conduct studies with compassion for their subjects. They shouldn't be cruel to show animals can be kind.

**References**

1. Contact Nobuya Sato. He coauthored a 2015 study in which rats displayed empathy and compassion by helping a drowning rat. Here is a description:

   > For their test of altruistic behavior, the team devised an experimental box with two compartments divided by a transparent partition. On one side of the box, a rat was forced to swim in a pool of water, which it strongly disliked. Although not at risk of drowning—the animal could cling to a ledge—it did have to tread water for up to five minutes. The only way the rodent could escape its watery predicament was if a second rat—sitting safe and dry on a platform—pushed open a small round door separating the two sides, letting it climb onto dry land.

Needless to say, the dry rats in this unpleasant experiment opened the door to rescue the swimming rat. We're not barbarians! The researchers even tempted us with chocolate behind another door. They thought we might eat the chocolate first, since it's delicious, but more often we let the swimming rat out first and then ate the chocolate. Because that's what lifeguards do.

2. Contact Inbal Ben-Ami Bartal, Jean Decety, and Peggy Mason. They conducted a 2011 study that confirmed rats feel empathy. A free-moving, untrained rat and a restrained rat were put in the same cage with chocolate (again with the chocolate!). Most often, the free rat taught themselves how to unlock the bound rat and then shared the chocolate. Mason wrote:

   > It said to us that essentially helping their cagemate is on a par with chocolate. He can hog the entire chocolate stash if he wanted to, and he does not. We were shocked.

   Correction: Rats helping rats is not shocking. What's shocking is the behavior of people—throwing us into pools and restraining us just to prove we care about each other!

3. Contact Satoshi Nakashima. He coauthored a 2015 study showing that rats recognize pain and suffering in the facial expressions and body language of other rats. Which is like, duh! Since humans can recognize nonverbal expressions of pain, why shouldn't rats?

   We agree with neuroscientist Jeffrey Mogil:

   > I would be more surprised if [rats] didn't have this ability. If it was only something we could do, we'd have trouble explaining where the ability came from. [Empathy in rats] makes evolutionary sense.

## Names Versus Numbers: Words Matter

When Marc first began studying animals, scientific practice was to label animals with numbers, not give them names. Most scientists believed animals did not have feelings or active inner lives, and numbers treated them that way—like inanimate objects in a warehouse.

Names imply that animals have feelings, thoughts, and a sense of self. That is what Marc has always believed, so he has always named the animals he's studied.

Words matter. They reflect who or what we believe animals to be. Throughout his career, Marc has argued that we must change our language to reflect the fact that animals are sentient, subjective beings like us.

For instance, when Marc refers to species who are not us, he often uses the terms *other animals* or *nonhuman animals*, since it's easy to forget that we are also animals. In this book, we use these terms throughout, though for simplicity, we also use *animals* by itself.

We also use subjective pronouns—like *he, she, they*, and *who*—to refer to individual animals, and not objective pronouns like *it*, *which*, or *that*.

This doesn't feel unusual with companion animals, whose individual personalities are self-evident. In other contexts, replacing objective language with subjective language can feel awkward and even startling.

Marc often says we should ask *who's* for dinner, not *what's* for dinner. The word *meat* is another example of objectifying language, along with *bacon*, *steak*, *chops*, and so on. These words refer to things, but these objects were once subjective beings—each a he or she.

People tend to use euphemisms and indirect language for animals in many contexts, like farming, hunting, research labs, and conservation. In part, this reflects our uncomfortable feelings about death, but with animals, it also sanitizes killing and denies subjectivity.

Animals are called *pests*, *livestock, game, prey, nuisance species*, and *invasive species*. And instead of *killing* (or *murder*, which we use only for people), we say *sacrificing, culling, removing, harvesting, bagging, disposing, eliminating*.

Pay attention to the language you and other people use when referring to animals and try to choose terms that respect their subjectivity.

## A Herd Leader Submits

Betsy was the unquestioned herd leader, dominant and ill-tempered.

The large, solid brown, bay quarter horse didn't tolerate equine challenges or novice riders. She was more than willing to threaten horses with her hooves or to return inexperienced riders back to the barn.

Then, one hot August day in 2004, while Betsy and three other horses were grazing in the pasture, a four-year-old boy scrambled under the wire fence, ran up to her in a jangle of limbs, laughed with delight, and tossed himself onto his back at her feet.

The boy was named Rowan, and he and his father, Rupert, had been on a walk. When Rowan saw the horses, he bolted before Rupert could stop him.

Rupert approached the fence cautiously. When horses feel spooked or threatened, they may defend themselves by kicking at or trampling the threat. Rupert knew of Betsy, which made him even more terrified.

Yet as boy and horse regarded each other, "something extraordinary" happened. Rupert says Betsy "dipped her head and mouthed her lips. The sign of equine submission."

Rupert, an experienced horse trainer himself, says, "I had never seen this happen. My son had some kind of direct line to the horse."

Or maybe it was the other way around.

### *A Heartfelt Meeting*

Rowan was not a typical boy. From a very young age, he'd showed signs of severe autism, and he'd been formally diagnosed earlier that year. He babbled instead of talking, made repetitive movements, didn't point or gesture, didn't show interest in others, and flew into frightening tantrums, Rupert says. These rages grew so extreme that Rowan would scream without stopping, bang his head on the ground, and even vomit.

Rowan's parents tried every intervention—including speech, occupational, and behavioral therapy, plus homeopathic medicine and various diets. The only thing that lessened Rowan's symptoms was walking in nature. And Rowan was obsessed with animals.

Rupert retrieved his son that August day, and they didn't return to the horse pasture for another six weeks. When they did, Rupert says Rowan "made a beeline for the old bay mare, the herd leader, Betsy." Again, Betsy submitted, licking and chewing her lips.

Rupert asked his neighbor if he and Rowan could ride Betsy, and the man agreed.

By putting his son on a strange horse, Rupert admits, "I broke all the rules." Though "famously grumpy with adults," Betsy's unusual restraint with Rowan made Rupert feel reassured.

The day Rupert prepared her to ride, this tolerance continued. Rowan ran wild in the barn, yelling, hitting the horse with dolls, chasing a cat, and racing beneath her belly. Through it all, Betsy "stood like a rock, moving not a muscle," Rupert says.

Rupert asked Rowan if he wanted to get up. "I wasn't expecting a response," he says, "but for the first time ever, he gave me an answer to a question. 'Up,' he said. And off we went."

To Rupert's amazement, the conversation continued as they rode. Rowan repeated his father's words, mostly mimicking, but Rupert says it was still "more cognitive speech than I'd ever heard him utter."

On impulse, Rupert urged Betsy to run, and Rowan laughed in ecstasy. Rupert was amazed at Betsy's responsiveness to his commands. "This was the first time I had ridden her. Yet already we had achieved a level of instinctive trust … that usually takes months, sometimes years, to build."

After the ride, Rupert asked Rowan to say thank you to Betsy. Immediately, Rowan hugged her brown head and gave her a kiss. "As he did so, an expression of extraordinary gentleness came over her," Rupert says, "a blissful half-closing of the eyelid."

Rupert says, "Something passed between them, some directness of communication that I, a neurotypical human, could never experience."

### *A Mysterious Connection*

Were Betsy and Rowan experiencing an intuitive connection that went beyond words? If so, what was it?

Seeking to understand this mystery, Rupert consulted with Dr. Temple Grandin, a professor of animal science at Colorado State University who also happens to be autistic.

Like Rowan, Grandin exhibited severe autistic symptoms as a child, and an early connection to horses helped lessen them.

Grandin told Rupert, "Animals think in pictures. So do I. So do many autists. It means we can't connect to other people, who think differently, in words or other mental patterns. Because animals think the same way—visually—autistic people often connect well with animals."

We don't know whether this is true or not. Experts in animal cognition dispute the idea that nonhuman animals and autistic humans think the same way. What can't be disputed is that Betsy chose to behave compassionately with Rowan, and Rowan, who barely acknowledged people, exhibited love and caring for Betsy.

Even if horse and boy didn't share a meeting of minds, they connected emotionally, and in ways we can only guess, it seemed related to Rowan's autism.

At one point, Rupert asked a teacher to help Rowan develop his language skills while riding Betsy. The teacher had an autistic son, who came along, and Betsy responded to her son with the same submissive gestures.

Further, Betsy's kindness didn't always extend to Rupert. He experienced her uncooperative nature whenever he tried to adjust her gait. He says that very occasionally, as a warning, she "gave her head a couple of annoying tosses." One time, she reared and knocked off father and son. Throwing Rowan seemed to shock her. Holding very still, she shivered as they remounted. Even more dramatically, one day the cinch broke and the saddle swung down, sending both Rupert and Rowan tumbling to the ground. Rupert twisted to cushion Rowan's fall, but his foot caught in the stirrup and his head slipped under the wire fence.

"When horses feel a saddle slip around like that," Rupert says, "they usually go into a fit of kicking.... [The] instinct is to bolt, bucking wildly, until the hated thing has been kicked off."

Rupert admits, "I should have been dead meat. But again Betsy did not move; she just stood there, with that soft look in her eye she always had when Rowan was on the ground near her." Rupert felt Rowan's presence saved his life.

After a long ride in spring 2005, Rowan threw a fit when the ride was over. Then, abruptly and unprompted, he stopped wailing, walked up to the horse, and hugged and kissed her foreleg, saying, "I wuv you, Betsy."

"It was the first time he'd ever said the words," Rupert says, and as always, "Betsy's eye half-closed as he held on to her."

### *The Limits of Equine Therapy*

Rupert Isaacson uses the "Horse Boy Method" with a client, Conquest Centre, Somerset, England, 2012. Photo by Adrian Sherratt/Alamy.

Rupert is quick to clarify several important points: There is no cure for autism, nor was he seeking one. In addition, for a long time, the behavioral changes Rowan experienced while riding only lasted while he was riding.

However, lessening Rowan's symptoms, even briefly, improved his life, so Rupert kept exploring what it is about meeting animals and riding horses that helps many children on the autism spectrum. Over time he founded two methods of equine therapy, called the Horse Boy Method and the Movement Method. Neither is centered around developing a particular relationship with an individual animal. Instead, they use animal encounters and the physical movement of horse riding to help bring symptoms under control.

Today, Rowan is an articulate high school graduate with the ability to manage his own symptoms; he no longer needs horse riding to do this.

Betsy's kindness, and Rowan's early relationship with her, was a critical part of this process. But Betsy is not unique. Many animals—dogs, cats, dolphins, horses, and so on—display caring for humans in emotional pain, and some individual animals pay particular attention to those who have physical, mental, or emotional disorders. When animals do this, their empathy and compassion are therapeutic in ways that heal from the inside and go beyond words or explanation.

## Learning to Read Signs

If animals could talk—using human language—what might they say? And if we could speak to animals using a shared form of communication—what might we tell them?

We don't have to wonder. With great apes, we've already done it. And they've already told us the most important things about themselves.

### *Washoe*

Apes can't vocalize like humans, but they have expressive hands. Since the 1960s, multiple research projects have taught great apes American Sign Language (ASL), and these experiments have revolutionized our understanding of our closest relatives.

In 1967, Washoe, a female chimpanzee, was the first nonhuman and the first great ape to learn ASL. She could eventually sign around 350 words and was clever about improvising her own. The first time she saw a swan, she signed "water" and "bird." This knocked one Harvard psychologist for a loop. He said it "was like getting an S.O.S. from outer space."

Well, maybe more like a wake-up call that, yes, other species can think and communicate. Now that dozens of great apes have learned ASL, we're not quite so stunned to find they're smart and sassy.

Washoe could be moody and spoiled, probably because she was doted on constantly. Whenever a researcher she worked with disappeared for a time—perhaps to take vacation—Washoe conveyed her annoyance by ignoring them when they returned. When this happened to research assistant Kat Beach, Kat apologized using sign but then decided to tell Washoe the truth.

"My baby died," Kat signed. She'd been away for several weeks while recovering from a miscarriage.

By then, Washoe had lost two of her own babies—one to sickness and one to a heart defect—and she'd been fascinated by Kat's pregnant belly and knew she was having a baby.

Washoe met Kat's eyes and signed "cry," then touched her cheek below her eye. When Kat was leaving that day, Washoe stopped her and signed "please person hug."

Washoe understood Kat's sorrow and cared, and using ASL, she conveyed both. So, what more do we really need to know about what chimpanzees think and feel?

### Chantek

Chantek was the first orangutan to learn ASL. Beginning in 1978, Chantek was raised in a human environment and taught by anthropologist Lyn Miles, who thought it would be "big news" if he could learn even one word. He eventually mastered over 150 signs. Chantek was a lovable scamp: He lied and deceived to get what he wanted; he knew the driving directions to his favorite ice cream and fast-food shops; and he strategized continual escapes, but only to explore the world and meet people (see "Wanted by the ZBI").

He never went far and he always returned because he was happy living with Miles.

Chantek communicated many thoughts and feelings, but his moments of empathy and compassion stand out.

After eight years with Miles, Chantek was moved to a primate research center. He was distraught and confused. For one thing, he'd come to think of himself as human. Through sign, he referred to himself as an "orangutan person" and to other orangutans as "orange dogs."

One day Miles came to visit and asked how he was doing. Chantek signed, "Hurt." When Miles asked where he was hurt, he signed, "Feelings."

Chantek signed for Miles to open the door. When she refused, he signed, "Get key." Miles signed that she couldn't, and Chantek signed, "Get car." When Miles signed, "Go where?" Chantek replied, "Go home."

About a decade later, Chantek was transferred to Zoo Atlanta, where he stayed until he died in 2017. While Chantek had to be retaught a lot of the sign language he'd known before, he never forgot how to sign "I love you," which he told Miles often.

Hannah Jaicks, a research student who worked with Chantek for a year, describes how she was busy one day and in a bad mood. She had cut her hand, which was wrapped in a bandage. As she struggled to set up her equipment, Chantek kept signing at her, but she was too agitated to listen.

"Finally," Jaicks says, "I stopped setting up the computer and snapped, 'What, what is it you want to tell me?' And he was signing to say he was sad. Still impatient, I said, 'Sad? Chantek, why, why are you sad? We need to work.' He signed back to me, 'I'm sad because you're hurt.' I'm pretty sure that was the most humbling thing that's ever happened to me."

Of course, dramatic moments always get our attention, but sometimes quiet encounters are even more revealing about who someone is.

One day at Zoo Atlanta, while Miles was working with Chantek in his open enclosure, it started to rain.

"Chantek had a bunch of materials in his enclosure," Miles says. "One was a long stiff piece of cloth, and he put it on his head. And then he looked out and he saw—I didn't have anything. I was getting wet. So, he took the cloth and he tore it in half. And he pushed it through the bars and he told me to put it on my head.

"And we stood there against the building, in the rain, and all Chantek signed was, 'Rain, rain.'"

Caring for the people we love in the smallest ways is what empathy and compassion are all about.

—

## Get Started: Humane Education—Compassion in the Classroom

Learning about nonhuman animals is certainly important, but *how* we learn, and *what we do* with our learning, is equally important.

That's the focus of what's called *humane education*. This teaches the intrinsic value of all animals, the interconnectedness of humans and nature, and the need to treat all animals humanely. In humane education, learning the essential values of kindness, empathy, and responsibility go hand in hand with learning about biology, ecosystems, and evolution.

We believe this is essential, and it's why we've written *Love in Their Hearts*. Marc dubs this "rewilding education," which he believes should also include getting kids out of the classroom to explore nature and observe wild animals directly—or exactly what Marc wanted as a child. The lesson we emphasize is simple: Animals have feelings and their emotions matter to them, and we need to translate that awareness into our daily lives and choices.

In this Get Started section, whether you are a student, a teacher, or a parent, we ask you to consider the way your school teaches about animals as well as how it cares for any animals within school, such as "class pets" and animals used for dissection.

When Marc was in high school, he refused to participate when animals were dissected. He says, "My teachers were not very open to this, but I refused to do it. Instead, I learned the same material through reading." In fact, concerns over animal welfare are slowly changing how biology is taught in medical schools and veterinary programs, many of which no longer use animals.

As you consider this issue, ask yourself if what you're learning about animals, the way you're learning, and how your school handles animals matches your own ethical standards. If something doesn't "feel right," think about it more closely and try to identify what you feel is wrong and what you wish were different.

Understanding and articulating our own ethics is a vital part of humane education and one goal of these Get Started sections. We learn how we want the world to be by identifying what causes harm and what we do and don't approve of. Then we consider if there are any actions we can or want to take.

It's very important to emphasize that every person and every situation is different. There is no one-size-fits-all solution to anything. That includes every issue raised in this book. You are the only one who can decide what feels right for you. Further, identifying a problem doesn't mean we can fix it nor obligate us to act. But naming a problem is the first step.

So, here are some ways we suggest approaching a problem you identify involving animal education and care in your school. These are ideas to consider, and you might find that none of them feel appropriate for you and your situation.

For more information about humane education, see the sources on Marc's website https://marcbekoff.com/love-in-their-hearts.

1. Decide how you feel and why, so you can explain what you consider harmful and what you want changed. Consider researching the issue, especially to brainstorm alternatives.
2. Ask friends and people you trust if they feel the same way. Others may raise issues you hadn't considered, and there's strength in numbers. Sometimes schools respond better when a group speaks.

3. If the problem is specific to a class, respectfully talk to the teacher. Express your concerns and offer alternative ways to learn the material without harming animals.
4. If the problem involves a shared curriculum or the school itself, talk to the school's administration. Again, express your concerns respectfully and offer alternatives.
5. If the response is dismissive or inadequate, consider your options. You might drop the issue, seek more opinions, offer other solutions, or broadcast your concerns to the larger community. You could start a petition among students, address a school board meeting, or contact local media.
6. If the harm is very serious, and you think the school is deliberately negligent, consider legal action. This isn't appropriate in most situations, but students have brought and occasionally won cases related to animal abuse at their schools.

# 3

# oh, what a wonderful world

## Curiosity, Wonder, and Awe

Giant Pacific octopus, Alaska SeaLife Center, Seward, Alaska.
Photo by Neibrugge Images/Alamy.

Science is about curiosity and asking questions with an open mind. Since many species exhibit curiosity, that makes them "citizen scientists," too.

Curiosity means being observant, attentive, and inquisitive, whether our focus is the world, others, or ourselves. We recognize curiosity by someone's rapt fascination, by their keen listening, smelling, tasting, touching, or watching. A curious animal uses all their senses.

Curiosity becomes wonder and awe when we're faced with a reality beyond our comprehension. And curiosity thwarted can lead to boredom, frustration, anxiety, and at its extreme, depression.

Judging by this book's stories, nonhuman animals feel the same way whenever they find themselves bored and trapped behind a locked door.

—

## Making Friends with an Alien

The creature has two eyes, three hearts, nine brains, one beak, and no skeleton or shell. All slimy body and muscle, it can squirt both black ink and a toxic skin-dissolving venom. Its own skin can change color and texture on a whim to mimic its surroundings or other deadly creatures. And its arms are covered in hundreds of suckers that can taste and are so strong they can pull up to a hundred times the creature's weight.

This one was named Octavia, and she wanted nothing to do with the humans gawking at her. A giant Pacific octopus, Octavia was like some sci-fi alien, an intelligent visitor from another planet. Like the fictional ET, she probably wished that, rather than be stuck in a temporary container at the New England Aquarium (their most recent arrival), she could return home to where she was born—the rocky Pacific Ocean floor off British Columbia.

One of the people crowded around was naturalist and author Sy Montgomery. Sy hoped to reach across a vast evolutionary divide—the modern octopus has barely changed in 200 million years, while modern humans arose only 300,000 years ago—and become friends with Octavia.

Sy wondered, "What might I discover about the interior lives of these animals if I were to use, as a tool of inquiry, not only my intellect, but also my heart? … Was it even possible for a human to understand the emotions of a creature as different from us as an octopus?"

Their first meeting failed. Octavia refused to interact. She remained at the bottom of her container as far from people as she could get.

Sy decided to try another day.

### *The Curious Invertebrate*

Octopuses are wickedly smart and highly emotional, but we can barely conceive of their inner lives. An octopus' eight arms contain about two-thirds of their neurons, and each arm can think and act independently. This is called "distributed intelligence," and it gives octopuses essentially nine brains.

Wild octopuses are explorers, inventors, and strategists. They camouflage constantly to mislead both predators and prey. Some carry two halves of coconuts or large clam shells while traveling so they can hide at will. They collect objects of all kinds to decorate their dens. Nor are they shy around divers, tugging at face masks and stealing cameras.

Philosopher and diver Peter Godfrey-Smith says he can't shake "the sense of mutual engagement that one can have with them. They watch you closely.… If you sit in front of their den and reach out a hand, they'll often send out an arm or two, first to explore you, and then—absurdly—to try to haul you into their lair."

They aren't hungry, just curious, which might be their defining characteristic. "It's been shown that octopuses are … interested in objects that they pretty clearly know they can't eat," Godfrey-Smith writes.

"In captivity," Sy says, "octopuses enjoy toys, often the same ones with which children play. Octopuses like to take apart and put together Mr. Potato Head. They play with Legos. They'll unscrew the lids to jars to get a tasty crab inside—but they enjoy manipulating objects so much, they'll often screw the lid back on when they're through."

Octopuses are notorious for escaping tanks, using brawn, brains, and the ability to squeeze through holes no larger than an apple. Sometimes, they sneak out at night to steal fish and crabs in neighboring tanks and return to their own tank by morning. They know people can see them. Unfortunately, octopuses can also die between tanks if they're out of water for too long.

Battling an octopus's boredom is a genuine problem for aquarium staff. Around 2000, about a decade before Octavia arrived, the New England Aquarium instituted regular touch sessions with people. No one knew if octopuses would enjoy this, "but we said to hell with it," one staff member explained. "The octopus is bored! Then we started playing with it."

### *Enjoying Each Other's Company*

The third time Sy visited Octavia, the octopus changed her mind.

After the container opened, Octavia rose to the top, and Sy says, "Her red skin signaled her excitement. I was excited too. She had my left arm up to the elbow encased in three of hers, and my right arm held firmly in another."

Despite Octavia's tremendous strength, her beak, and her venom, Sy says, "I felt no threat from Octavia. I felt only that she was curious." Sy describes her bulbous head as "silky and softer than custard."

Since "octopuses can taste with their entire bodies," Sy felt Octavia "knows me in a way no being has known me before."

By tasting Sy's hormones, Octavia could discover a lot: her emotions, that she was female, what she'd had to eat or drink, even medications. Octopuses sometimes react negatively to smokers; perhaps the taste of nicotine is gross.

After this encounter, Sy visited Octavia regularly for months, and each time, "Octavia rose to the top of the tank and flowed over to meet me, eager to taste me with her suckers and look me in the face."

All they did was touch. "Octavia enjoyed me, I think, because we liked to play with each other. Our games … were more like versions of patty cake, but with suckers."

One time, right before Sy left to travel, they had their longest hug yet. Sy says:

> She held on to me, gently but firmly, for an hour and fifteen minutes. I stroked her head, her arms, her webbing, absorbed in her presence. She seemed equally

attentive to me. Clearly, each of us wanted the other's company, just as human friends are excited to reunite with each other. With each touch and each taste, we seemed to reiterate, almost like a mantra: "It's you! It's you! It's you!"...

While stroking an octopus, it is easy to fall into reverie. To share such a moment of deep tranquility with another being, especially one as different from us as the octopus, is a humbling privilege. It's a shared sweetness, a gentle miracle, an uplink to universal consciousness.

Sy plays with Sy, a friendly giant Pacific octopus named after her at the New England Aquarium. Photo courtesy of the New England Aquarium.

When Sy returned from her trip, Octavia had been moved to the aquarium's main tank, where she lay an enormous clutch of eggs. Sadly, the eggs were sterile. They would never hatch, but Octavia devoted all her energy to them as if they would. She stopped interacting with people and focused solely on protecting her most important creation.

At the same time, she began to die. For female octopuses, hatching their offspring is their last task. Mothers forego food and everything else until then, for as long as it takes, and pass away soon thereafter.

Almost a year later, the aquarium removed Octavia from the main tank. She was by then an "old lady" and near death.

After so long apart, Sy and Octavia met one last time. Sy says, "Her wet grip on my skin felt gentle and familiar, the pull of her suckers tender as a kiss." She and the other aquarium staff interacted with Octavia for about ten minutes, and "we knew in that moment that Octavia had not only remembered us and recognized us; she had wanted to touch us again."

After Octavia returned to the bottom, Sy remembers, "I leaned over the barrel and stared at her in awe and gratitude. My eyes brimmed, and a tear dripped into the water."

Sy wonders if Octavia might have tasted that tear.

Sy says:

> Being friends with an octopus—whatever that friendship meant to her—has shown me that our world, and the worlds around and within it, is aflame with shades of brilliance we cannot fathom—and is far more vibrant, far more holy, than we could ever imagine.

## Roots & Shoots: Passion in Action

Jane Goodall's Roots & Shoots is a wonderful model for how to make the world a better home for everyone—humans, animals, and nature. The well-being of the planet depends on widespread efforts to care for all of Earth.

Roots & Shoots began in 1991 when a group of local youngsters gathered on the front porch of Jane Goodall's home in Tanzania and talked about how they felt powerless against the world's problems. As the students told stories and offered ideas, Jane realized the solution was right in front of them: their power to create change.

In that moment, the "roots and shoots" concept was born. As Jane put it:

> Roots creep underground everywhere and make a firm foundation. Shoots seem very weak, but to reach the light, they can break open brick walls. Imagine that the brick walls are all the problems we have inflicted on our planet. Hundreds of thousands of roots and shoots, hundreds of thousands of young people around the world, can break through these brick walls.

Today, Roots & Shoots programs exist across the United States and around the world, and they total over two hundred thousand members, ranging in age from kindergarten through college. Specific projects focus on local communities, and they are based on a four-step formula:

1. Get inspired: Identify what you're passionate about, what issues face your community, and what you enjoy doing.

2. Observe: Figure out what your community needs to solves issues and how you specifically can help.
3. Take action: Develop a plan based on your research and do it!
4. Celebrate: When finished, evaluate your impact, celebrate your accomplishments (including simply taking action), and reflect on how to improve next time.

For more than twenty-five years, Marc has been an ambassador for Roots & Shoots and led events—many with Dr. Jane, as people called her—all over the world. In 1999, Marc helped found the first group in his hometown of Boulder, Colorado, at an elementary school. One popular project they originated, called "Dreams and Hopes," was inspired by Dr. Martin Luther's King's famous "I Have a Dream" speech. Students are asked to complete the phrases "I have a dream that _____" and "I am thankful for _____," and then they make drawings based on their responses.

Marc has led many groups and helped lots of young people pursue their projects. In 2024, Marc helped seventh-grader Bastian Wrede join Roots & Shoots. Bastian founded Wolf Defender (http://wolfdefender.org) and created a mobile app called "Howl: For the Wolves" to raise money for and awareness of wolf conservation.

Bastian told Marc:

> I have always loved wolves, maybe because we had a dog when I was little, named Rowdy, that looked like a gray wolf. Then as I got older, I learned more about them and read about plans to kill them rather than ensure they remain part of our world. I decided I wanted to do something to help and so I created Wolf Defender.
>
> I believe that my project will find its greatest success through micro-activism. To me, this is people working in their own communities to benefit their local organizations under the umbrella of a common goal. For me, Roots & Shoots is the perfect way to meet passionate people in other places and work with them to support wolf conservation in their communities.

## Wanted by the ZBI

The Zoo Bureau of Investigation (ZBI)* periodically publishes citizen warnings related to captive animal escapes. In the interests of public safety, the ZBI is circulating these historical most-wanted posters of three legendary orangutan escapists. While these individuals have passed, the ingenuity and determination of orangutans lives on. Thankfully, orangutans almost never leave zoos nor act violently. Orangutan experts say their motivations are various: They sometimes escape their enclosures out of frustration or boredom, to eat ice cream, to have fun, and/or to meet people. Another motivation seems to be that they are cunning engineers who can't resist solving the puzzle of locks.

Should any member of the zoo-visiting public discover an orangutan free of their enclosure, please report this immediately to the nearest ZBI agent. Even if the orangutan is sitting quietly and posing for selfies, they should be considered hairy-armed and extremely devious.

---

* *Authors' Note:* These wanted posters are fake. The ZBI does not exist, since zoos aren't jails meant to punish lawbreaking animals. But these orangutans are real, and every detail about their escapes is true. We don't know what any zoo animal understands about being caged, but these stories should make us wonder: If orangutans are this smart, do they experience confinement as unfair, like punishment for crimes they can't understand? Most of all, should we respect their relentless efforts to escape, whatever their motivations, by not confining them in zoos in the first place?

# CHANTEK

AKA: "The ape who went to college"

*Serial escapist, felony fence dismantling, misdemeanor coed startling*

## REMARKS

Born in captivity and raised as a human; unaware that he is an orangutan; given carpenter's tools for his birthday and learned how to use them; works alone; familiar with American Sign Language, so ASL can potentially be used for negotiations; has sweet tooth that's useful for bribes; knows driving directions to fast-food restaurants.

## CAUTION

The escape artist Chantek will roam if given the slightest chance. During the period when Chantek lived on campus at the University of Tennessee—Chattanooga with his trainer, Lyn Miles, the campus police kept Coke and M&Ms in their vehicles to bribe Chantek. Typically, once bribed, Chantek comes quietly.

Summary of incidents:

- While living in the same trailer as Miles, Chantek secretly unraveled the chain-link fence separating his living space from hers over several days, then trashed the trailer when Miles was out.
- Frequently jumped the fence that surrounded the yard outside the trailer. If not caught first, he returned home himself after pranking the student body.
- Once free, he would hide near sidewalks and jump out to startle students into dropping ice cream or other food, then eat the food himself.
- Also known to pretend he needed to pee. If unwary students led him to a bathroom, he would choose the woman's side and lock himself inside a stall. When an unsuspecting female used an adjacent stall, he would waggle his arm beneath the barrier to make them scream.
- After transfer to Zoo Atlanta, Chantek immediately started dismantling his cage and escaped multiple times. When zoo officials contacted Miles for advice, she said, "Just give him hamburgers so he'll sit." This worked.

# FU MANCHU

AKA: "honorary member of the American Association of Locksmiths"

*Felony group escape, criminal bartering, padlock destruction, misdemeanor wire concealment*

## REMARKS

Known for a friendly, easy-going manner and insatiable curiosity; fathered twenty children; as a child himself, climbed inside parkas of keepers to play with them; former keepers warn is "single-minded" about escape.

## CAUTION

Fu Manchu's early escape attempts mostly involved tearing apart padlocks and locking mechanisms. His place on the ZBI's most-wanted list is due to a series of high-profile, extremely clever escapes at the Omaha Zoo. No escapes have been recorded since, but vigilance is key.

As best as can be reconstructed, Fu Manchu bartered with a female orangutan, trading food for a piece of wire she had previously stripped from a light fixture. Why she did this, how the negotiations unfolded, and whether Fu Manchu already knew how to use the wire to open a door are unknown. Lacking pants or pockets, Fu Manchu kept the wire hidden in his mouth, holding it between lip and gum.

Thus, regular dental hygiene might have prevented this episode.

At some point, Fu Manchu used the wire to unlatch a furnace-room door, which was accessible from the orangutan enclosure. The furnace led to a set of stairs that exited into the zoo grounds.

During the first escape—all occurred when the zoo was closed to the public—keepers were alerted to Fu Manchu and four other orangutans in the trees by the elephant barn. Days later, keepers again found the same group of five miscreants wandering free. The head curator assumed human error and was, quote, "ready to fire someone."

The zoo set up surveillance, and when Fu Manchu led a third group escape, he was caught red-handed. Which, it should be noted, is the only way to catch a red-haired orangutan.

# KEN ALLEN

AKA: "the Hairy Houdini"

*Serial escapist, felony taunting and crude gestures, impersonating a zoo ambassador*

## REMARKS

Born in captivity in the San Diego Zoo; a bad influence on fellow orangutans by encouraging their own escape attempts; irritable with orangutans he dislikes; when loose, tends to sit in front of exhibit entrance, greeting people, shaking hands, and letting himself be petted; usually returns to enclosure willingly.

## CAUTION

ZBI agents should be aware that Ken Allen's notoriety has made him a so-called "folk hero." Zoo visitors are known to cheer when he flees zoo employees attempting to corral him. He has a fan club selling "Free Ken Allen" bumper stickers, and he is glorified in song ("The Ballad of Ken Allen"). Agents should not be misled by this public affection; he is a relentless escapist. Further, he is known to give zoo visitors, regardless of age, the finger. Presumably, he understands this gesture.

Summary of incidents:

- As an infant, in a display of remarkable ingenuity, he regularly unscrewed the bolts of his cage at night, explored the nursery, and put everything back together, with himself inside, by morning.
- On his second escape, he approached another orangutan enclosure and threw rocks at Otis. This was, apparently, in retaliation for an unresolved beef from when they were enclosure-mates.
- Once used bamboo to construct a ladder and escape.
- Once was observed by staff holding an overlooked crowbar, tossed it aside as if he didn't care, but threw it in range of a fellow orangutan, who later, unseen, grabbed it to jimmy open a window to get them both out.
- When electricity was cut to fix a pump, he realized the electric fence was off and climbed out. Always ensure equipment is accounted for and in working order. Orangutans are always watching.

## The Great Rain, the Mighty Waterfall

Physically and behaviorally, humans and chimpanzees are almost the same. We share over 98 percent of genes and around 90 percent of expressions and gestures—like kissing, shaking fists, swaggering, back slapping, and holding hands.

As anthropologist Frans de Waal has said, chimpanzees are "equally evolved," and "their socio-emotional lives resemble ours to such a degree that it is unclear where to draw the line."

One line some people draw is spirituality. They say only humans experience wonder and awe—that we alone ever contemplate being an ephemeral drop of consciousness in the eternal ocean of the universe.

However, in their own ways, might chimpanzees sometimes ask who made them and all of nature? Might they feel an urge to celebrate and express the miracle of being alive? Might they stand mute before the divine mystery of existence itself?

And if they do, how would we recognize it?

### *Dancing in the Rain*

At Gombe National Park in the 1960s, Jane Goodall watched chimpanzees eating in a fig tree on a dreary spring day:

> At about noon the first heavy drops of rain began to fall. The chimpanzees climbed out of the tree and one after the other plodded up the steep grassy slope toward the open ridge at the top.... As they reached the ridge the chimpanzees paused. At that moment the storm broke. The rain was torrential, and the sudden clap of thunder, right overhead, made me jump. As if this were a signal, one of the big males stood upright and as he swayed and swaggered rhythmically from foot to foot, I could just hear the rising crescendo of his pant-hoots above the beating of the rain. Then he charged off, flat-out down the slope toward the trees he had just left. He ran some thirty yards, and then, swinging round the trunk of a small tree to break his headlong rush, leaped into the low branches and sat motionless.

One after another, the other six males followed: running downhill, breaking branches and hurling them, then swinging themselves into trees. Meanwhile, the audience of females and children watched from the ridgetop. Then the males trudged back up the slope and did it again—and yet again—as, Jane said, "the rain fell harder, jagged forks or brilliant flares of lightning lit the leaden sky, and the crashing of the thunder seemed to shake the very mountains."

This "rain dance" lasted for twenty minutes, and the performance was as dramatic as the storm. As Jane later discovered, individual chimps often do this, but group displays are rare, and rain dances are reserved for those sky-opening deluges when, as we might say, "the heavens part."

Whatever the chimpanzees are thinking, uncontained nature clearly evokes a swirl of uncontainable emotions, inspiring behavior that mimics a deliberate, self-aware ritual.

As the group finally left that day, Jane said, "One male paused, and with his hand on a tree trunk, looked back—the actor taking his final curtain. Then he too vanished over the ridge."

### *Drumming in the Forest*

A male chimpanzee and two females doing a pant-hoot, Gombe National Park, Tanzania, 2012. Photo by Fiona Rogers, Nature Picture Library/Alamy.

Chimpanzees are known to drum. Researchers think they do this to define territories or attract a mate and that these patterns might be precursors to musical rhythm. But what if chimps also drum for the same reason we make music—to express our passions through rhythm, vocalization, and movement?

Biologist Caitlin O'Connell describes the strange ritual called "accumulative rock throwing." This behavior has been observed only among male chimpanzees in West Africa. O'Connell says that, after the chimp carefully selects a fig tree with a hollow, resonant trunk, the performance begins:

> Suddenly, the chimpanzee stands and picks up a rock the size of a melon. His shoulders start heaving and his lips purse as he emits a soft moaning sound. The moaning gets louder and louder, shorter and sharper in a buildup that reaches an open-mouthed climax—the chimpanzee's signature pant-hoot vocalization.
>
> At the height of this intense call, the chimpanzee reveals his intention and hurtles the rock against one of the buttresses of the tree with a bang. He then climbs onto the buttress and briefly beats at it with his feet as if he were playing a drum.... After a good drumming, he runs off into the forest, screaming.

Sounds pretty punk, actually.

### *Worshipping the Waterfall*

Jane Goodall witnessed another remarkable chimpanzee ritual that, as much as any, seems to embody a genuine nature-related spiritual experience.

Here she described a chimpanzee approaching a waterfall in a heightened state of arousal:

> As he gets closer, and the roar of the falling water gets louder, his pace quickens, his hair becomes fully erect, and upon reaching the stream he may perform a magnificent display close to the foot of the falls. Standing upright, he sways rhythmically from foot to foot, stamping in the shallow, rushing water, picking up and hurling great rocks. Sometimes he climbs up the slender vines that hang down from the trees high above and swings out into the spray of the falling water. This "waterfall dance" may last ten or fifteen minutes.

Jane asked, "Is it not possible that these performances are stimulated by feelings akin to wonder and awe? After a waterfall display the performer may sit on a rock, his eyes following the falling water. What is it, this water?"

### *Watching the Sunset*

At the Gombe Reunion 2003 in Minneapolis, Minnesota, Jane Goodall performs a pant-hoot along with the audience of researchers. Photo by ZUMA Press, Inc./Alamy.

From the outside, a spiritual experience can look like nothing. For a period of time, someone lies down, kneels, sits, or stands, yet inside they feel moved in ways that are hard to explain.

Might that very stillness be another sign of awe?

Like us, chimpanzees are known to admire the sunset. For ten minutes or more, individuals may pause whatever they are doing. Groups will gather, greet, and sit on a particularly good lookout as the sun signs off for the night.

Are the chimpanzees admiring beauty? Are they enjoying a peaceful connection to nature? Or are they thinking about what to eat for dinner?

These chimpanzees aren't doing anything, but *something* is going on inside. And we'd be foolish to assume that an animal's curiosity can't lead to the biggest questions of all.

Ecologist Carl Safina writes:

> Many other animals are curious, and human curiosity is a precursor to wonder, which is a precursor to spirituality, which is a precursor to science. Science seeks to find out what's really going on. And science's searching is everlasting wonder.

## Childhood Inspiration: Breanna Locke

As a teenager, Breanna Locke found a home with Jane Goodall's Roots & Shoots program. Today, she is a book editor at Shambala Publications, a spiritual publisher seeking to foster a kinder world, which includes our relationship with animals.

> For sensitive kids, the lone vegetarians at their cafeteria table, it's easy to feel insignificant and like the plight of the world is outside their control. For them, finding Roots & Shoots can be like a salve that turns anxiety into agency and empowers them with a newfound community of support. I know that was the case for me.
>
> Like many animal-loving little girls, I grew up idolizing Jane Goodall. When I first learned of her life with the chimpanzees—via a National Geographic special playing on the overhead projector in elementary school—I was entranced. There she was, a living, breathing example that an individual could turn a personal kinship with animals into a life of action to make real, positive impact. Years later, as a teenager, I got to see my hero speak at a lecture in Boston, and that's where I first learned of Roots & Shoots. A group for young people aimed at helping animals and the environment? This kind of involvement is what I had been hungry for, and I knew I had to join.
>
> I found the nearest group in Holliston, Massachusetts. It was inspiring to witness the positive contributions kids were making to the world already at such a young age. We did activities and fundraisers for environmental-related causes. My favorite was a yearly dog wash we organized to bring in funds for a local humane society. When I attended the Roots & Shoots Global Youth Summit, I was introduced to an even larger pack of like-minded young adults that I hadn't realized even existed. I wasn't a weird, lone vegetarian in this crowd like at high school—these were my people!
>
> The sense of community and agency I gained in Roots & Shoots seeped into other areas of my life as I grew up. I am so proud to be an alum, and I am continuously in awe of all that Roots & Shooters continue to contribute to our world. Cheers to the next generation of changemakers!

## Get Started: Unleashing Your Pet

This chapter tells stories about wild animals, but every sentient being is curious. They have active minds, and they want to explore their world and satisfy their needs. This includes domestic animals, whose lives are often very restricted. Even companion animals (or pets) can wind up spending a lot of time confined, alone, and bored.

To get started improving the lives of animals, the easiest and most effective way is to focus on any animals who share our home. We need to do everything we can to give our household companions the most fulfilling, enriching, and healthy lives possible.

So, it's time, as Marc likes to say, to "unleash your pet." We know that sounds like chaos but let us explain.

A good life for anyone means more than plenty of good food, exercise, and loving attention. Every being wants the freedom to make *their own* choices and do what *they* want.

Many dogs, for instance, want to play with every dog they meet, sniff every blade of grass, and chew as much as possible. People usually don't have patience for that, and we get frustrated when dogs act like dogs. Instead, we train dogs not to pursue their desires and call them "good" when they don't.

But they're only being "good" from our perspective. For a dog, even when they cooperate, they are still being denied what they really, really, really want.

"Unleashing your pet" means providing companion animals with as much personal freedom as possible. It's one of the best gifts we can give them.

This is true for dogs as well as lizards, cats, fish, parrots, hamsters, and so on. A good life for any species includes the freedom to satisfy their needs on their own terms; that's one lesson of the "escapist" orangutans. Of course, we can't let companion animals run loose in our homes and cities all the time; cages, tanks, and leashes can be necessary. But a life lived only in a cage is no life at all.

In the book *Unleashing Your Dog*, which Marc cowrote with bioethicist Jessica Pierce, they list ten ways to care for dogs, and these can be applied to any companion animal:

1. Let your animal be themselves.
2. Teach your animal how to thrive in human environments.
3. Be open to what your animal can teach you.
4. Be attentive to the unique challenges faced by your animal.
5. Make life an adventure for your animal.
6. Give your animal as many choices as possible.
7. Make your animal's life interesting by providing variety in feeding, walking, and making friends.
8. Give your animal endless opportunities to play.
9. Give your animal affection and attention every day.
10. Be loyal to your animal.

The bottom line is to consider the world from your animal's perspective and try to give them what they want as much as possible. Every species is different, so this requires some research. Plus, every individual is different, so pay attention to your companion animal's likes and dislikes.

As just one dog example, take chewing. Dog expert Paul McGreevy once told Marc, "To chew is to be a dog." So let your dog chew—by teaching them what and when they are free to chew to their heart's delight. One strategy is to fill a rubber chew toy with dinner, so they have to work for their meal.

Humane educator Zoe Weil often says, "The world becomes what we teach." We also could say, "Companion animals become who we teach them to be." We need to teach them well, and when we do, it's a win-win for all. Our relationships with pets must include give-and-take, mutual respect, tolerance, and lots of love.

Taking an animal into our lives is a huge responsibility. Unleashing them gives them more freedom to express who they truly are in and for themselves.

# 4

# under pressure

## Fear, Anxiety, Pain, and Worry

Jasper the moon bear relaxing on his hammock.
Photo courtesy of Animals Asia.

Like us, animals can be worrywarts. They get stressed and anxious about all sorts of things.

Marc says, "I've shared my home with a number of dogs who paced around nervously, hid under the bed, wrapped themselves in sheets, and lost sleep when there were severe thunderstorms."

Not all animals like to dance in the rain!

Research has shown that almost all sentient animals, even insects, experience and try to avoid pain. What we don't know, and may never know, is what that experience is like for nonhuman animals.

When it comes to animal emotions and intelligence, some scholars and researchers try to quantify differences among species. But these comparisons are not very useful; they are fraught with errors and practical challenges. With emotions, there's currently no way to directly and meaningfully measure them among nonhuman animals. While there appear to be differences, the distinctions are turning out to be less than we think.

When it comes to pain and animal welfare, some people still ask: Do pigs suffer more than chickens? Or fish more than lobsters? Or humans more than other animals?

The truth is that each individual's pain is *their* pain.

Even if we estimate the most intense pain for individuals of one species is half what it is for individuals of another species, that's still the most extreme pain for both. From the individual's perspective, suffering is suffering.

This is why differences among species is never a reason not to care for nonhuman animals as best as we can.

—

## Cow #6490

In 2012, researcher Kathryn Gillespie visited Ansel Farm—a pseudonym—to explore up close what life is like for a dairy cow.

After arriving, she was met by a ranch manager, Homer Weston—also a pseudonym—who escorted her into the large dairy barn. About five hundred Holstein and Jersey cows were divided among several pens.

As they approached the maternity pen, Gillespie says, "a small Jersey heifer with ear tag #6490 walked up to me and stretched her head out, neck extended over the fence."

She continues:

> Gently, she reached out her long gray and pink tongue and licked my arm. Her large brown eyes, long eyelashes, and fuzzy cap of reddish brown hair were hard to resist, and I reached out to scratch her neck and behind her ears. She licked me again. Curious, other cows started to crowd around and, soon, [I was] petting and scratching and being licked by a small herd of cows who crowded at the fence.

The cow with ear tag #6490 on a western Washington dairy farm. Photo courtesy of Kathryn Gillespie.

Cow #6490 was about two years old and visibly pregnant. She was due to give birth to her first calf in a few weeks. However, instead of a happy event, this would instead start the endless cycle of pregnancy and milking that would define the rest of her existence. Like all mammals, cows only produce milk to feed their young, so to keep cows producing milk regularly, farms must keep them almost continually pregnant.

The life of a dairy cow is hard and includes lots of stress, pain, and anxiety: Many dairies practice dehorning and tail docking (partial amputation of tails). There are common diseases like mastitis (an infection of the udders). Artificial insemination is the usual reproductive method. And physical pain ranges from sore legs and even lameness from standing on concrete floors to each cow's arrival in the slaughterhouse—once they are "spent," or their ability to produce milk diminishes.

Perhaps worst of all? Cow #6490 wouldn't be given a chance to mother a single one of her children.

### *A Society of Childless Mothers*

Once labor began, Cow #6490 would be moved out of the maternity pen, and after delivery, Homer said, "We take the calves out pretty quickly—you know, within a day, usually—and we have a separate farm where we raise the heifer calves until they're ready to come back here."

Some farms, especially megadairies with upward of ten thousand cows, don't wait that long. They separate calves within an hour.

We don't have to guess how mothers feel about losing their newborns. Homer said, "The cows'll bellow for the calves—like they're looking for them—for a couple of weeks a lot of the time."

Agitated displays of longing can continue for over a month, and we have no idea if the feelings ever end, especially since the separation of mother and calf gets repeated every year and for every cow in the barn.

Author Jeffrey Moussaieff Masson describes one incident that was told to him:

> When the calf was first removed, [the cow] was in acute grief; she stood outside the pen where she had last seen her calf and bellowed for her offspring for hours. She would only move when forced to do so. Even after six weeks, the mother would gaze at the pen where she last saw her calf and sometimes wait momentarily outside of the pen.

The common wisdom among dairy farmers is that quicker is better. Homer told Gillespie, "The longer they bond, the harder the separation is." This is undoubtedly true, since, as Masson writes, "familiarity breeds love."

This begs a question: What does endless separation breed, especially when the experience is shared by everyone you know?

After they give birth, cows are milked for about three months before they are impregnated again, and they give birth after about nine months. Typically, about two months before delivery, cows are separated from the main herd and not milked, which means they produce milk for about ten months a year.

During that time, they have nothing to do but be milked, since they are not allowed to raise the next generation. That is, be mothers.

### *In Business, Survival Means Efficiency*

To get milk from a cow, immediately separating mothers from calves isn't required. It's a choice, and it's always been done. Even Shakespeare wrote about it:

> *And, as the Dam runs lowing up and down,*
> *Looking the way her harmless young one went,*
> *And can do naught but wail her darling's loss.*
>
> —Henry VI, Part 2

So why is the business run this way?

Because the economics of dairy farming requires maximizing the amount of milk they produce. The farm must be as efficient as possible to survive financially. Even farms that value animal welfare over maximizing profits separate mothers from calves eventually, though not as quickly.

Further, as Gillespie emphasizes, the farmers themselves usually care for and even love their animals. During his tour, Homer continually showed genuine concern and affection for his charges. It's just that the needs of business tend to trample the emotional welfare of everyone, including the people doing the work.

This is hard to acknowledge. Do cows experience fear, worry, anxiety, and grief? Absolutely. They have signaled that on dairy farms for centuries. Even if it makes us uncomfortable as we shop in the grocery store, we can't deny their emotions.

Gillespie says, "If the heifer with ear tag #6490 at Ansel Farm continued on to a routine life trajectory for cows in the dairy industry, her life will have been better than most cows used for dairy production." Still, the "somber reality" of her life "nagged at me as I patted the heifer … and scratched behind her ear once more, in parting."

## Anthropomorphism: How We Talk about Animal Emotions

> *I have learned that anthropomorphism is a deeply suspect word, used to defend cruelty to creatures unable to speak and defend themselves against human exploitation.*
>
> —Sir Brian May, founding member of Queen and the Save Me Trust

The term *anthropomorphism* means attributing human characteristics, feelings, and intentions to nonhuman animals. For a long time, fear of this led some scientists to believe that we should never describe the feelings of nonhuman animals using human terms—and maybe that we shouldn't characterize their thoughts and feelings at all. That's because, in the past, the majority of scientists remained skeptical those feelings existed.

To avoid mistakenly projecting our feelings onto animals, researchers were supposed to describe only external behavior. They could describe an animal's physical gestures and postures, but without using emotional language. The most they could say was that animals were acting "as if" they had feelings—as if, were they human, we'd call them happy, sad, or angry.

This misguided caution is not just unnecessary but misleading.

First, the only way we can describe anything is using language. Words are inexact, but they're the only tool we've got. In everyday life, most people describe animals using emotional language—because it's clearest and most direct.

For example, no one would say, "Watch out! That dog's lips are pulled back to show his teeth, the hair across his shoulders is erect, and he is vocalizing in a lower tone, behaviors that, if he were human, we'd associate with anger."

No. Growling, bared teeth, and raised hackles almost always signal anger—unless a dog is playing—and that's what we say: "Watch out! That dog looks angry!"

Second, and more importantly, we know sentient animals have inner lives. Animals don't act "as if" they feel; they do. Our challenge is to understand and describe those feelings as accurately as possible. For that, we need all our words.

Third, research confirms, as this book shows, that many sentient animals share a range of similar emotions—as evidenced by similar behaviors, expressions, social relationships, brain structures, hormones, and neurochemicals. We aren't imagining it when animals express emotions we recognize, since we're all animals.

Fourth, and most interesting of all: Many animals display empathy—or an intuitive ability to identify the feelings of others—and they display this ability across species. To be clear, we don't mean empathy as in "sympathize with" or caring. We mean simply recognizing the emotional state of another being. Empathy itself suggests that recognizing emotions, rather than being an anthropomorphic error, might reflect a very practical, effective, nonverbal capability many animals are born with.

Having said that, it's easy to be wrong. For lots of reasons, we can misinterpret or misidentify the emotions of nonhuman animals. We can fail to see critical gestures, misunderstand behaviors, or not recognize the social context. Our different sensory capacities might not pick up the smells or sounds that other animals are reacting to or communicating with. We might self-servingly presume that our experience must be what others experience or that animals feel whatever we wish or hope they did.

Inaccuracy is always a danger. There are a few ways to guard against this. One is knowledge, or the detailed study of the minds, emotions, and behavior of animals.

Another is remembering that *similar* doesn't mean *the same*. The key is to always consider the animal's point of view—their unique circumstances, their different senses and selves. It means remembering that a dog who acts happy or jealous isn't understanding situations or experiencing emotions exactly as we do. Marc calls this *biocentric anthropomorphism*, which means using the tool of human language to capture another being's experience as best we can.

While it's impossible to get emotions right every time, the bigger mistake is to deny animal emotions out of fear of getting them wrong. Anthropologist Frans de Waal called this *anthropodenial*.

In fact, maybe our urge to anthropomorphize simply reflects the power of the human-animal bond. It's a sign of our deep, mutual connection, which doesn't need words to be communicated or understood.

## Wildlife Guide: Stranger Things

Given what we know about animals, it's tempting to assume that every single living being on Earth must be sentient, or capable of feeling. The truth is we *really* don't know.

We might never be certain for *all* creatures.

It's only recently that researchers have even bothered to ask if Earth's strangest and tiniest beings feel anything. What about scallops, jellyfish, dragonflies, ants, snails, spiders, mosquitoes, and other beings with brains the size of poppy seeds?

This wildlife guide takes a quick look at some of the unexpected and undeniably strange creatures we have been able to confirm display some type of sentience—though we still know next to nothing about their actual inner lives.

So far, this has mostly come from studies on pain, stress, and fear. One reason studies focus on this is because it's easier to tell when a creature doesn't like something and adjusts their behavior to avoid it. But also, if we confirm that species feel pain, that impacts questions of animal welfare.

### *Crustaceans and Cephalopods*

In a 2021 report, philosopher Jonathan Birch and his colleagues developed a framework of eight criteria for evaluating the existence of sentience in other animals. Their criteria focus on the capacity to experience pain, distress, and suffering.

Using this, the researchers reviewed the existing scientific literature related to crustaceans and cephalopods—primarily octopuses, squids, shrimp, crabs, lobsters, and nautilus. After examining over three hundred papers, they confirmed that every species satisfied some if not all criteria. As a result, they recommended that all these species "be regarded as sentient animals for the purposes of UK animal welfare law."

A year later, the British government extended its laws to do just that and added octopuses, lobsters, and crabs.

What are the eight criteria?

The first three relate to the way the brain works. The fourth is how the animal reacts to the presence of anesthetics or painkillers. The fifth is making what's called "motivational trade-offs" between the cost of experiencing something unwanted to get something desired—that is, the relative willingness to endure pain to feel pleasure. The sixth is behavioral flexibility in response to injuries or threats. The seventh is associative learning, or remembering what happened before and acting differently because of it. The eighth criterion is valuing or seeking pain relief when injured.

These are interesting behaviors to keep in mind whenever you observe any animal, even dogs, cats, and birds. Knowing some things to look for, can you recognize when animals are avoiding and managing painful experiences?

### *Fish*

We've known fish experience pain and fear for at least two decades. In her classic book *Do Fish Feel Pain?*, fish expert Victoria Braithwaite concluded, "I have argued that there is as much evidence that fish feel pain and suffer as there is for birds and mammals—and more than there is for human neonates and preterm babies."

More recently, we're discovering that fish have surprisingly complex emotions. Did you know that seahorses are romantic fish, and mated couples will dance for hours?

Biologist Lynne Sneddon, another fish expert, once conducted a series of experiments with zebrafish that clearly showed some of the eight criteria above. First, she let zebrafish choose where to live: either in a barren aquarium with nothing or an attractive tank with gravel, plants, and views of other fish. Naturally, the fish preferred a well-decorated home. Then Sneddon injected some fish with acid and flooded the empty aquarium with painkillers—and those fish headed straight for the boring tank that now eased their pain.

Then she made one more test: She injected painkillers into the fish in pain, so they felt better no matter where they swam, and what do you know? Those fish returned to the enriched aquarium. The zebrafish preferred an interesting home but were willing to give it up if that soothed what hurt.

### *Reptiles*

A Jamaican iguana, Hellshire Hills, Jamaica. Believed extinct for nearly half a century, this lizard has made an incredible comeback. Photo by Joey Markx, courtesy of the International Iguana Foundation.

A variety of reptiles display complex parenting behaviors and even like to play. We've long known reptiles are sentient, and yet people rarely notice or appreciate how much captivity in small tanks can cause stress.

Reptile biologist Clifford Warwick has identified several behaviors that indicate stress, including hyperactivity, passivity, head-hiding, inflation of the body, hissing, panting, pigment change, and other abnormal behavior patterns. For example, a reptile might be stressed if they inflate their body. These are useful ways to assess any pet reptiles.

### *Insects*

Consider this: Scientists calculate that the world's total biomass of insects is well over twice the biomass of humans. Plus, while we've identified nearly a million insect species, there might be tens of millions. No matter how hard we try, we'll never know if every insect feels. There are too many of them and too few of us.

However, sentience among insects is turning out to be, potentially, far more widespread than we thought. In 2022, researchers decided to use the eight criteria developed by Jonathan Birch and others to evaluate insects. They scoured the existing scientific research related to six insect orders and found "strong evidence for pain" in all manner of flies, mosquitoes, cockroaches, and termites, and they found "substantial evidence for pain" among all types of ants, bees, wasps, butterflies, moths, grasshoppers, crickets, and more.

Significantly, the authors wrote, "We found no good evidence that any insects failed a criterion."

Lots of recent research has focused on bees, since human agriculture depends on these important pollinators, and if bees suffer, we might starve. Entomologist and ecologist Stephen Buchmann writes: "Bees are self-aware, they're sentient, and they possibly have a primitive form of consciousness. They solve problems and can think. Bees may even have a primitive form of subjective experiences."

Bees not only get depressed but can show symptoms that resemble PTSD (post-traumatic stress disorder), which can occur when humans and nonhuman animals experience severe trauma.

In this "bee scrum," male bees fight in a life-or-death struggle to be the first to mate with a virgin female bee. Photo courtesy of Dr. Stephen Buchmann.

Philosopher Bob Fischer, the director of the Society for the Study of Ethics & Animals, has also reviewed the existing research on insects. He says, "When my team tried to compare the experiences of insects and other animals, we found differences but not huge ones. I think we underestimate insects."

As we say, from an evolutionary perspective, feelings are useful—they're what biologists call adaptations. They help us survive. Given how successful insects are, it would make evolutionary sense if many were sentient and had emotional lives of their own.

Bob admits: "I was pretty skeptical of insect sentience at one point; I didn't think that insects mattered. But the more I've learned, the more I've come to care about them."

## Jasper: The Spokes-Bear for Forgiveness and Hope

*Here, Marc shares the story of Jasper, a moon bear (or Asiatic black bear) who was rescued from a Chinese bear bile farm:*

I dedicated the first edition of my book *The Emotional Lives of Animals* to Jasper. I have always considered him an ambassador for forgiveness, generosity, peace, trust, and hope. Honestly, I consider all moon bears, and every animal who is able to recover from abuse, to be ambassadors to us, but Jasper holds a special place in my heart. We must listen carefully to the lessons these animals teach us and incorporate them into our lives.

I met Jasper and learned about the terrible practice of bear bile farming because of my friendship with Jill Robinson, who founded Animals Asia to save bears like Jasper. The bile of moon bears is an ingredient used in traditional Chinese medicine (as well as in cosmetics), and even though there are plenty of herbal and synthetic alternatives, this practice continues.

Jasper arrived with a group of sixty-three bears at the Moon Bear Rescue Centre outside of Chengdu, China, in 2000. Jill and the wonderful humans who work with her receive bears from bear farms after the animals are no longer useful to the farmers. Bears usually arrive in horrible condition, suffering from serious physical and psychological trauma. Each bear is given a complete physical and a psychological evaluation. Many need surgery. After they've acclimated to the center, some bears have to be kept alone, whereas others can be introduced to other bears.

When I first met Jasper, I could feel his gentle kindness. His omniscient eyes said, *All's well, the past is past, let's go and move on.* Jasper's gait was slow and smooth as he approached me. I fed him peaches out of a bucket and gave him peanut butter. His long, wiry tongue glided out of his mouth as he gently lapped the tasty treat from my fingers. I could tell Jasper was a remarkable being.

Here is the story Jill told me about when she learned about the plight of moon bears:

> It was April 1993. A journalist friend urged me to visit a bear bile farm in China. I was intrigued and nervous, having never visited such a place, and knowing nothing about the species of Asiatic black bears or about the bear bile industry.

About a week later, I joined a group of Japanese and Taiwanese tourists and entered the farm. The farmer and his wife were boasting outside their shop about everything their bile could cure. As many people began to buy the bile products, I took the opportunity to sneak away and find the victims of bile extraction. I found a doorway leading to a basement where the caged bears were kept.

Absolutely nothing prepared me for that moment. Thirty-two moon bears stared forlornly out of their "crush cages" and made nervous, popping vocalizations every time I approached them—clearly anticipating something terrible was going to happen.

As I looked more closely, I knew why they were afraid—years of cage confinement saw scars running three to four feet in length along their bodies, teeth smashed from repetitive and frustrated bar biting, others with teeth and paw tips deliberately cut away to make them less dangerous to handle, and worst of all, metal catheters poking out from infected holes in their abdomens, from where their bile was milked.

Never had I felt more shocked or helpless, sick to my stomach with the reality of what these creatures had suffered over decades of being exploited. Suddenly I felt something touch my shoulder and turned around in shock to see a female moon bear reaching her paw through the cage.

At that moment, it seemed simply right to take her mighty paw in my hand, and rather than hurting me, as she could have done, she squeezed my fingers. Her message was clear. I knew instinctively I'd never see her again—but that moment saw a promise that bear farming would one day end.

That moment was responsible for the founding of Animals Asia in 1998, the construction of a sanctuary in Chengdu and another sanctuary in Vietnam. This is why I will never forget that very first bear—her name was Hong.

Crush cages are torture devices. The top can be lowered by half to flatten bears so they can't stand or move while the bile is extracted. Imagine being pinned in a phone booth and all you can do is turn your head to drink water and eat, while a rusty metal device is inserted into your abdomen. Imagine this happening for years, then decades. Some bears have been imprisoned for thirty years.

This is the most extreme type of fear, anxiety, and mental distress anyone could endure, which is epitomized by a story reported by the Chinese media in 2011. When a captive moon bear heard her son cry out in pain as a catheter was inserted, the mother became uncontrollable and broke free, causing the staff to run away in fear. The bear ran to her cub and smothered him, and then she ran headlong into a wall and died.

Heartbreaking stories like this are why I consider Jasper a spokes-bear for forgiveness and hope. Not only did Jasper survive, he became one of the happiest, most-loving, and most-playful bears at the center—the heart and soul of the sanctuary.

When abused animals play, this indicates that they've substantially recovered from trauma. When I visited the Moon Bear Rescue Centre in October 2008, I watched Aussie and Frank frolicking on a hammock. Jill and I shared their joy as we laughed at their silly antics. When Aussie saw Jasper ambling over, he jumped off the hammock, approached Jasper, and they began roughhousing—caressing one another, biting one another's scruff and ears, and falling to the ground in an embrace. Tears came to my eyes. These bears were telling one another that they were okay. Whatever trauma they'd experienced wasn't stopping them from enjoying themselves and spreading that joy. Traumatized animals don't play, nor are they outgoing like these awesome bears.

Jasper was a peacemaker who gently interrupted conflicts among bears, as if reassuring them. Jasper truly opened his heart to everyone he met, and I think he knew the effect he had. He could also be a rascal. Jill said he was a "photobomber" and always butted in whenever visitors took pictures of the bears. If you didn't know what Jasper had been through, you would never have guessed from his behavior and spirit.

Sadly, Jasper passed away in 2016, having developed a liver tumor to which his abuse on the bile farm might have predisposed him. Ultimately, he lived fifteen years on a bile farm and fifteen years in the sanctuary.

I often wonder what qualities allowed him to recover, when others don't. Was he special? Bears, like many animals, have different personalities. As friendly as he was, Aussie would still run back into his den when he heard a strange noise. As an ethologist, I always want to learn more about each individual being—what they feel, how they travel through life, how they keep their dreams alive.

Jasper the photobomber poses for a photo. Photo courtesy of Animals Asia.

I wonder what the rescued moon bears carry in their heads—what remnants of abuse and trauma remain? Perhaps they talk about how lucky they are to have been rescued. Perhaps they share that not all humans are bad, that some can be trusted.

I can't thank Jasper enough for sharing his journey and his dreams. His example helps inspire us to be more humane and thus more human. Jasper's spirit reminds us of our true spirit, our inborn nature, which is to help rather than harm.

## Childhood Inspiration: Camilla Fox

Camilla Fox has dedicated her life to the animal and environmental protection movements. In 2008, she founded Project Coyote, a national nonprofit that protects North America's wild carnivores and promotes compassionate coexistence between people and wildlife through education, science, advocacy, and coalition building.

> From a very young age, I had an affinity for wild nature and animals. I became a vegetarian when I was six years old after visiting my grandparents in northern England and visiting a nearby sheep farm. It was a bucolic farm in the Derbyshire moors, and it was my first time getting to bond with baby lambs. That evening, we went back to my grandparent's house, and I smelled an odd, unfamiliar odor wafting from the kitchen. I asked my grandmother what the smell was, and she said that she was cooking baby lamb. I was horrified. I said to my family that I did not want to eat the baby lamb, and I never wanted to eat meat again, and that was that.
>
> I am blessed to have had parents who instilled in me an appreciation for other beings, be they winged, furred, or scaled. I'm also incredibly grateful that they allowed me to follow my own path, including my decision to not consume animals. My mother rescued and rehomed cats, and we always had many in the house—generally the "rejects," too old or infirm for adoption.
>
> My father studied the behavior of wolves, coyotes, foxes, and domestic dogs. We took in an orphaned wolf pup—a full timber wolf—before her eyes opened, when she was just six days old. She imprinted on us, and we became her pack for the next fourteen years. It was an amazing and indescribable experience to grow up with a wolf; she had such intelligence, sensitivity, and awareness.
>
> I feel incredibly fortunate to be able to dedicate my life and passion to charitable work for the voiceless—for the underdogs—and to fostering compassionate coexistence and appreciation for wildlife and wildlands.

## Get Started: Our Compassion Footprint—Who and What We Eat and Buy

We've all heard of our "carbon footprint." That refers to the amount of carbon dioxide and other greenhouse gases emitted into the atmosphere due to human activities. When it comes to helping nature and animals, Marc prefers to imagine our "compassion footprint." Rather than focus on the harm we do, our compassion footprint focuses on the good, which definitely feels better.

As many of this book's stories show, how animals are treated by society—in agriculture, industry, research, entertainment, and elsewhere—can cause them a lot of pain, fear, and anxiety, and some animals never fully recover from the trauma of extreme abuse.

While changing society is obviously important, we can also grow our compassion footprint by focusing on the personal choices in our everyday lives. In particular, we want to highlight two things that everyone does almost every day: eat and get dressed. Every choice we make about food, clothes, makeup, and other products can potentially improve the lives of animals.

In this case, our advice for getting started is simple: Eat less or no meat. Buy fewer or no animal products.

Let's look at both more closely.

### *Vegetarianism and Veganism*

Vegetarianism typically means not eating meat, while veganism means not consuming any animal products, like milk, cheese, and eggs. Neither choice is solely about diet. Veganism is a philosophy (and sometimes part of religious practice) that seeks to avoid all forms of harm—to animals, land, water, and air.

Marc says, "Around 1990, I became vegetarian, and a decade later, I became vegan. I just did it—I call it 'going cold tofu.'" Marc explains, "I believe a 'vegan ethic' isn't radical. It's a way of living that touches numerous other areas, including culture, food production and ecology, politics, environmentalism, and economics."

Vegetarianism and veganism are growing in the United States, among both adults and children. And while many people still eat meat, attitudes and diets are changing to consume more ethically. Journalist Michael Pollan coined the term "conscientious omnivores" for this varied, middle-of-the-road group. This approach strives to eat less meat while trying to source all food from more organic, ethical, and humane producers.

Expanding our compassion footprint doesn't mean doing something we don't want to do, and not everyone wants to be vegetarian or vegan. Plus, for young children like Camilla Fox, who decided not to eat meat when she was six years old, parents need to support their child's choices. As we say throughout, everyone's circumstances are different, and we each have to decide for ourselves what actions feel right for us.

It's also easy to get caught up in labels and feel that, if we aren't perfect, we've failed or our efforts don't count. Our compassion footprint isn't defined by any single action or choice. Rather, it represents our ongoing efforts to do better, be better, be more thoughtful, and improve our choices so we avoid harm to animals as we seek a kinder world.

### *Dressing Ethically in Style*

For many years, groups like People for the Ethical Treatment of Animals (PETA) have advertised the harms of the fur industry and of animal testing in cosmetics. These efforts have worked, and many products now promote themselves as "cruelty-free," and many people no longer wear fur.

Today, the term "ethical fashion" refers to much more than avoiding specific animal-based products. The focus is on using consumerism to help address the overall impacts of the fashion industry.

There is no better example of this than Emma Håkansson, the founder of Collective Fashion Justice. In an interview with Marc, Emma described the current sustainability ethic in fashion as "sterile and lifeless" because few people address the interwoven problems throughout the supply chain—from the suffering of the sheep whose wool is gathered, to the suffering of the workers who make the clothes, to the environmental impacts of production and distribution.

Emma said, "There is a need to consistently consider people, our fellow animals, and the planet alike. Our key campaigns focus on shifting the fashion industry beyond the use of animal-derived materials. It is in these supply chains where all three are harmed, and so all three can benefit from this progress."

Whenever our personal choices can address animal justice, environmental justice, and social justice all at once, we are truly expanding our compassion footprint.

# 5
# at home with the blues

## Sadness, Grief, and Depression

Three male elephants stand over the dead body of Polly after her tusks had been removed by rangers. Photo courtesy of Dr. Joyce Poole, Scientific Director ElephantVoices.

Charles Darwin, keen observer of animal emotions, provided this tutorial in close observation:

> I formerly possessed a large dog, who, like every other dog, was much pleased to go out walking. He showed his pleasure by trotting gravely before me with high steps, head much raised, moderately erected ears, and tail carried aloft but not stiffly....

Darwin then described how the dog's manner changed whenever they detoured in an unwanted direction:

> His look of dejection was known to every member of the family.... This consisted in the head drooping much, the whole body sinking a little and remaining motionless; the ears and tail falling suddenly down, but the tail was by no means wagged.... The eyes changed in appearance, and I fancied that they looked less bright. His aspect was that of piteous, hopeless dejection.

Darwin found the dog's reaction "laughable, as the cause was so slight." Yet this amusing anecdote embodies an important truism: If animals feel joy and happiness, they must experience the opposite.

The blues come in many shades. We can be glum, wistful, disheartened, despondent, anguished, and miserable; we can feel melancholy, woe, discontent, depression, and despair.

While these stories plumb the depths of sadness, it can be oddly comforting to know we aren't the only ones who experience grief and sorrow.

—

## Elephant Funerals

> Intelligent, social, emotional, personable, imitative, respectful of ancestors, playful, self-aware, compassionate—these are qualities that would gain most of us membership to an exclusive club. They also describe elephants.

So says ethologist, conservationist, and famed elephant expert Cynthia Moss, who has closely studied elephants for over fifty years. The club she refers to is the one we founded when we believed humans were the only ones who qualified.

Not anymore.

As evidence that elephants belong in "our" club, Moss has witnessed one of the most compelling and mysterious aspects of elephant society: their fascination with the dead and their funeral rituals.

Moss describes one such encounter:

> They stood around Tina's carcass, touching it gently.... Because it was rocky and the ground was wet, there was no loose dirt; but they tried to dig into it ... and when they managed to get a little earth up they sprinkled it over the body. Trista, Tia, and some of the others went off and broke branches from the surrounding low brushes and brought them back and placed them on the carcass.... By nightfall they had nearly buried her with branches and earth. Then they stood vigil over her for most of the night and only as dawn was approaching did they reluctantly begin to walk away.

It's not easy to bury an elephant. Even trying indicates deep emotion. We can only guess, from an elephant's perspective, what purpose this serves. It's not practical. A light covering of dirt and plants won't keep scavengers away. As with us, burial is surely a gesture of mourning, a way to acknowledge someone's passing. It expresses our grief both individually and as a community.

The first time Moss witnessed an elephant burial was during her study of the Echo family. Several elephants encountered the dead remains of an unfamiliar female. As they examined the elephant, Moss says, they "began to kick at the ground around the carcass, digging up the dirt and putting it on the body. A few others broke off branches and palm fronds and brought them back and placed them on the carcass."

Then a plane flew overhead, circling lower, and the elephants ran away. It was the park warden coming to recover the tusks. At the time, Moss speculated that "if they had not been disturbed, they would have nearly buried the body."

Years later, she discovered she was right.

### *A Skull-and-Bones Society*

Elephants don't always bury the dead. Sometimes they surround a carcass and simply touch and examine it, displaying prolonged, sensitive attention. Still, burials have been observed enough times to confirm that they aren't unusual. They occur even among captive elephants.

Elephantine curiosity with death and the dead doesn't stop there.

Famous elephant expert Joyce Poole writes:

> Elephants are particularly interested in tusks and may carry them long distances before dropping them, but they also carry other bones. I once watched an elephant walk off with a newly collected lower jaw that was part of a scientific assemblage. Other naturalists have observed an elephant returning bones to the original site of an animal's death, and moving and burying scores of elephant feet and ears that were drying after a culling operation.

Moss has seen this, too. She watched a group of elephants stop to examine some elephant bones on the ground: "Some elephants begin to turn the bones over and pick them up in their trunks, feeling their nooks, crannies, and crevices. It's the detailed exploration of the bones that is so striking—all while the elephants, at least some of them, vocalize."

Others have observed female elephants, while examining bones, secreting fluid from glands at their temples, which typically occurs during moments of stress and high emotion.

Researchers have tried to figure out what elephants understand. Can they tell the difference between elephant bones and those of other species? Do they prefer the skulls of elephants they know?

Indeed, elephants easily distinguish and prefer elephant bones over others, and while they sometimes prefer the skulls of known elephants, not always.

Elephants are probably trying to figure out who died as they sniff skulls, but more than that—death moves them.

Top left: An elephant, Polly, as she is dying, still sitting up in the grass.
Top right: Polly as she fell over and passed away.
Bottom: Two of the three male elephants who visited Polly and tried to revive her after she died.
Photos courtesy of Dr. Joyce Poole, Scientific Director ElephantVoices.

### *Grief Is the Other Side of Love*

When elephants stand vigil, Poole writes, "It is their silence that is most unsettling. The only sound is the slow blowing of air out of their trunks as they investigate their dead companion. It's as if even the birds have stopped singing."

For us, grief expresses how much we care and how hard it is to accept that someone we love is gone.

As Poole writes, elephants seem to share this reaction:

Tonie standing over her stillborn baby. Joyce Poole told Marc: "I brought water to her in a basin, and at one point, I was pouring as she was drinking—her tusks inches from my head. Later, she touched me on my chest with her trunk." Photo courtesy of Dr. Joyce Poole, Scientific Director ElephantVoices.

> Some years ago, I witnessed the death of an elephant named Polly and watched as three males spent an hour trying to raise or revive her. Using their trunks, they tried to pull her up by her own trunk, her tusks, and her tail; with their tusks and their feet they tried to lift her.... Two days later, after rangers had hacked Polly's long, asymmetrical tusks from her face, I returned to find the same three males standing side by side, touching her mutilated face with their trunks, undoubtedly able to detect the hand of man. They were deeply engrossed in their investigation, and I had the horrible realization that on some level they understood the connection between Polly's wounds and the missing tusks.
>
> On a couple of occasions, I've seen very real grief on the faces of elephants. The first time was when I watched a young female, Tonie, stand guard over her stillborn baby for three days. The first day she tried over and over to revive him by lifting him with her trunk, tusks, and forefoot. Then, she simply stood by

> him. Throughout, her face and body expressed what I recognized from my own experience as grief. Her head, ears, and trunk drooped, the corners of her mouth turned down, and her movements were quiet and slow. I knew that Tonie was experiencing a deep sense of loss.

Dame Daphne Sheldrake, another legendary elephant advocate, has said that elephants "grieve and mourn the loss of a loved one just as deeply as do we, and their capacity for love is humbling."

—

## Wildlife Guide: Animals in Mourning

This wildlife guide presents a few of the many species who exhibit grief and engage in mourning behaviors. If you ever encounter animals reacting to a corpse, watch closely. What do they do, and what do those actions seem to indicate about what they feel and think?

People once believed only humans understood death and grieved, but the opposite seems true: Most animals seem capable of recognizing death, and when someone they love dies, it matters deeply.

Animal researchers use several criteria to identify death-related emotions. For instance, do animals show unusual attention or concern for the dead individual, perhaps examining or covering the body or gathering in a group vigil? Do animals exhibit consoling behaviors with each other, like staying close, vocalizing, or using physical gestures? Do animals act in unusual ways or change routines—becoming agitated, eating or sleeping less, isolating, and so on?

Sometimes grief is unmistakably intense—such as when mothers carry their dead children for days or weeks at a time. On rare occasions, animals have died from grief.

Susana Monsó, a philosopher who studies animal minds, suggests that most animals seem to display a "minimal concept of death," which is that the dead individual no longer functions and that "this is an irreversible state."

Beyond that, what animals understand about death remains a mystery.

### *Ducks*

Anthropologist Barbara King tells the story of two rescued male ducks, Kohl and Harper. They had been abused, were in bad shape, and were "very afraid of people," King says. "Kohl had deformed legs and Harper was blind in one eye."

For four years, the friends bonded in a way that was unusually close even for ducks, who are very social. One day, when it became too painful for Kohl to walk, he was euthanized, and Harper was allowed to watch. Afterward, he approached his dead friend.

"After pushing on the body," King says, "Harper laid down and put his head and neck over Kohl's neck. There he stayed for some hours."

Harper was unable to recover. For two months, he ignored the other ducks and spent all his time sitting near the pond where he and Kohl had played, until he himself passed away.

### *Magpies*

Marc has witnessed numerous animals mourning. Several have been accidental encounters near his Colorado home. Marc says:

> Many years ago, I was riding my bicycle with my friend Rod when we witnessed a very interesting encounter among five magpies. Magpies are corvids, a very intelligent family of birds. One magpie had obviously been hit by a car and was lying dead on the side of the road. The four other magpies were standing around him. One approached the corpse, gently pecked at it—just as elephants will nose a carcass—and stepped back. Another magpie did the same thing. Next, one of the magpies flew off, brought back some grass, and laid it by the corpse. Another magpie did the same. Then all four magpies stood vigil for a few seconds and one by one flew off. I'd never seen anything like this before. At the time I hadn't read any accounts of grieving magpies. Rod agreed with my impression. We both felt these birds were clearly saying a magpie farewell to their friend.

Since then, numerous people have told Marc about other corvids, like crows and ravens, performing mourning rituals for their dead companions.

### Foxes

*Here Marc describes a fox burial:*

One morning a neighbor told me about the carcass of a red fox on the side of the road. I went to look at it. The fox, a formerly very healthy male, had obviously been killed by a mountain lion, whom I had accidentally met the night before. The fox's body was partially covered with branches, dirt, and some of the fox's own fur.

Later, when I was hiking along the road with my dog Jethro, I saw a small female red fox trying to cover the carcass. She was deliberately orienting her body as she kicked debris with her hind legs so that it would cover the dead fox, perhaps her mate. A family of foxes had lived near my house for almost a decade. She'd kick dirt, stop, look at the carcass, and intentionally kick again. I observed this "ritual" for about a minute. Afterward, the female continued to slink around the carcass with her tail down. A few hours later, I returned to the carcass and found it totally buried.

Had I just seen a fox funeral? Her actions and manner certainly reflected sadness and grief. I was lucky to see what I did. Much happens in the complex lives of animals that we can't see—and will never be able to re-create in a lab. When we're fortunate to observe animals at work, these splendid events can reveal much about their innermost feelings.

### Zebras

One day at the Mushara waterhole in Etosha National Park, biologist Caitlin O'Connell noticed a family of zebras. At first she paid them little attention, but by evening she realized they hadn't left or separated all day. The next morning, they were still together.

Then one of the zebras fell down.

> As soon as the zebra collapsed, the entire family held their heads down and looked on as the zebra lay flat out and motionless. They seemed to know that

this was no nap. It quickly became clear to me why they had stayed all this time—to stay with their sick family member.

Occasionally, one of the older females nuzzled the dead zebra and stamped a foot, another pawed the ground, and a few others bobbed their heads up and down. There was a whinny every now and again, but nothing—no response. The zebra had breathed its last breath.

Reluctantly, the herd eventually left the waterhole, and O'Connell says that it "made me think about how difficult it must be for all social mammals to make the hard decision to leave a fallen family member and move on."

A herd of zebras drinking at a waterhole in Etosha National Park, Namibia.
Photo courtesy of Thomas D. Mangelsen, Images of Nature.

### *Giraffes*

In Kenya in 2010, researchers observed a herd of giraffes reacting to the death of a four-week-old calf, who had been born with a deformed foot.

For two days, the calf's mother, along with anywhere from fifteen to twenty-two other female giraffes, hovered around the place where the calf lay dead. During the first day, the giraffes approached, nudged, and examined the carcass before retreating a short distance and behaving in a restless, vigilant manner. They huddled even more closely around the dead calf at night.

On the third day, the researchers found the mother sitting alone. About fifty yards away, they found the calf's half-eaten body. On the fourth day, hyenas came and took the rest away.

The researchers didn't speculate about what the giraffes were feeling, but for days, the herd's females were clearly trying to protect the dead calf from predators. There might be other explanations, but it sure looked like mourning.

### *Dolphins*

Death-related grieving has been observed in at least twenty species of cetaceans. In particular, dolphin mothers are well-known for their mourning displays over a dead infant.

Marine biologist and conservationist Maddalena Bearzi writes, "A dolphin mother may remain close to the floating, lifeless body of her dead newborn for hours, sometimes days, constantly trying to lift her offspring toward the surface with repetitive and anxious movements. She will often touch the lifeless body with her flippers and rostrum in a last hope to revive and breathe new life into it."

In 2001, a dolphin mother was observed in the ocean carrying a dead infant for five days. Other dolphins even helped her carry the body and drive away scavenging seagulls. In 2007, a researcher reported a similar incident that lasted two days. In that case, no dolphins directly helped the mother, but several stayed close, observing her.

Bearzi says a dolphin mother "never abandons her calf, not even to replenish herself with food. Her devotion is unselfish and unfaltering. A grieving dolphin mother may seek seclusion, away from her group, but in this time of grief, she might be visited by a group of her peers, perhaps coming to check on her, as we humans often do when someone we know is bereaved."

### *Killer Whales*

One of the most heartbreaking and public examples of animal mourning was the killer whale Tahlequah, who in 2018 carried her dead calf above the water for seventeen days. It was impossible for the world not to notice and grieve with her.

Tahlequah was part of a killer whale population off of San Juan Island in Washington. As the days passed, and the body steadily decayed, Tahlequah continued her vigil. Other pod members took turns holding the carcass, allowing Tahlequah to rest and eat, before she returned to take her dead calf back. Ultimately, Tahlequah traveled a thousand miles before letting the body go in what whale researcher Ken Balcomb called "a very tragic tour of grief." Amazingly, in September 2025, Tahlequah did this again, carrying another dead calf for over eleven days.

Scientists are still sometimes reluctant to identify less-dramatic behavior as grief, but occasionally, animal passions are too obvious to deny.

—

## A Sorrow Beyond Tears

In the 1870s, someone shared a story told to them by the keeper of the Philadelphia Zoo. Among the chimpanzees was a very closely bonded pair, and when the female died, the male tried to wake her up. When he couldn't, the person wrote, "his rage and grief were painful to witness.... The ordinary yell of rage ... finally changed to a cry which the keeper of the animals assures me he had never heard before ... *hah-ah-ah-ah-ah*, uttered somewhat under the breath, and with a plaintive sound like a moan."

The inconsolable male continued moaning like this for two days.

Chimpanzee mothers have occasionally been observed carrying their dead infants—like the stories of dolphins and killer whales. In one extreme case, a chimpanzee mother wouldn't release her dead, decaying child for over two months.

Grief is cathartic. It helps us process our pain and recover from loss. In the moment, it can feel like we'll never recover, but we do, even if a sense of loss remains.

Then again, some individuals don't recover. Jane Goodall witnessed this among the chimpanzees in Gombe National Park when a son, Flint, lost his mother, Flo.

### *Flint and Flo: An Unusually Strong Dependency*

The elderly matriarch Flo with her son Flint on her back. Photo by Hugo van Lawick.

A good mother who gave birth to five children, Flo was the matriarch of their chimpanzee community. Yet one of her sons, Flint, refused to launch into adulthood.

From birth, Flint was doted on and indulged by his mother and three older siblings. Flo was extremely attentive and would come running to cradle, kiss, and suckle him if he made even a peep of distress.

When Flint was around three, Flo tried to wean him, but this failed spectacularly. When Flint was denied, he flew into "terrible tantrums," Goodall wrote, "hurling himself about on the ground, flailing his arms, rushing down the slope screaming." With a look of resignation, Flo "plodded in pursuit to reassure her son and suckle him."

Their conflicts escalated. Flint started to bite and hit Flo when she refused to suckle him, and Flo hit and bit him back. Yet she always gave in.

When Flint was four, Flo became pregnant again, but nothing changed. Flint slept in Flo's nest, rode on her back, and whimpered if she stopped grooming him for a second. "We really felt sorry for old Flo," Goodall wrote. Despite her swollen belly, she had to carry "the half-grown male body of Flint, perched ridiculously on her frail old body."

Goodall speculated that "Flint's prolonged infancy was possibly due to Flo's extreme age," since she lacked the strength to force Flint to wean.

To Goodall's surprise, however, after the birth of his little sister, Flame, "Flint's behavior was exemplary." He groomed and cuddled Flame and stopped pestering his mother for attention. Nevertheless, over the next six months, Flint slowly reverted to his previous ways until he again "became Flo's baby."

In 1970, in the "Family Postscript" of her famous book *In the Shadow of Man*, Goodall listed the things she looked forward to learning as they established a permanent research center at Gombe. One of them was: "What happens to Flint when his mother actually dies?"

### *A Loss Too Large to Bear*

In 1972, Goodall found out when Flo, the troupe's fifty-year-old matriarch, passed away. By then, Flint was eight and a half years old. Goodall wrote:

> All day [Flint] sat near [Flo's] body at the edge of a small, fast-flowing stream. Occasionally he approached her, inspecting her carefully, moving all around, then grooming her a little. He pulled her dead hand toward him, whimpering; in life she had responded, grooming him in return. Then he moved a few yards away to sit, hunched and motionless, eyes staring. As darkness fell, Flint climbed into a tree and made a small nest—to spend the first night of his life alone.
>
> On the second day Flint heard his brother calling in a nearby group, and he joined them. Some of his depression lifted for a while, but after a few hours he suddenly left the other chimps and hurried back to the place where Flo had

died. There he sat alone, eyes staring into space. Later he climbed slowly into a tall tree, walked along a branch, and stood staring at a large empty nest—the one that Flo had made and that he and she had slept in the previous week. What was he thinking? He climbed down and lay on the ground, staring at nothing.

Over the next three weeks, Flint became increasingly lethargic. He stopped eating, and he avoided other chimps, huddling in the vegetation close to where he'd last seen Flo. His eyes sank deep into the hollow sockets of his skull; his movements were like an old man's. The last short journey he made, with many pauses, was to the very place where Flo's body had lain. There he remained, sometimes staring and staring into the water, until he died, just three and a half weeks after losing Flo. He died of grief.

—

## Captive Dolphin Depression Syndrome

The real-life story of Flipper is a tragedy.

In movies and on TV, the character of Flipper is a pop-culture icon. He's the aquatic Lassie, a fun-loving, free-swimming, smart, chattering, caring, wild bottlenose dolphin who always protects and saves his human friends.

A happy hero with a permanent smile, Flipper first swam to fame in the 1960s—appearing in two films and a four-year TV series—and he later returned in the 1990s.

It would be easy to confuse the fictional animal with the real thing because dolphins possess the same qualities. They are playful, highly intelligent, self-aware, deeply emotional, and intuitive communicators who are legendary for saving people from danger and death—from drowning and from sharks (see "Dolphin Versus Shark").

Yet the real dolphins used in entertainment are not free. And over the years, their unnatural lives as captive performers can undermine their sense of self and steadily lead to severe depression.

No one knows this better than dolphin expert and renowned activist Ric O'Barry, who trained all five dolphins who played the original Flipper.

### *How to Train a Dolphin*

As a teen, O'Barry always wanted to work with dolphins. He got his wish in 1962, when he was hired by the Miami Seaquarium.

Taught how to train by mentor Ricou Browning, who helped create the Flipper movies, O'Barry discovered training was simple: "You didn't feed them unless they did a trick.... Trainers call it 'positive reward,' but from the dolphin's perspective, it's called 'food deprivation,' and that is what it is."

Known as operant conditioning, this stimulus-and-response technique is based on behaviorism. Through repetition, dolphins learn that a hand signal is requesting a specific action (say, to leap), and performing the action results in being fed, which is the "reward" for cooperating.

"It may seem simple," O'Barry says, "but it wasn't." The dolphins had to deduce what each hand signal meant, and the same signals were often used for different things. One dolphin, Kathy, who played Flipper 90 percent of the time, "almost invariably got it right," O'Barry says. "In fact, she often knew not only what I wanted her to do but what I *should* have wanted her to do; in other words, there were times when I told her to do something wrong because I was confused but she did the right thing anyway."

Ric O'Barry with Kathy on the *Flipper* TV show set. Photo courtesy of Ric O'Barry.

As O'Barry soon discovered, dolphins are not just smart but sensitive. On the one hand, a full dolphin often won't perform, since they have no incentive—so dolphins are almost never fed before a training session or performance.

But they can't be starved into performing either. If dolphins feel mistreated, they also refuse to play along. O'Barry learned to approach training like teaching, in which he needed "the learner's cooperation."

O'Barry says, "If I was a good trainer, it was because of one talent I may have had in more than average amounts: empathy."

A caring, even loving relationship fostered the best training, and O'Barry pursued that with all his heart.

"I ate with the dolphins," O'Barry says. "I slept with them.... When they were hungry, I fed them. When they were sick or injured, I cared for them. When there was a new trick to learn, I taught them.... If I sound like a mother hen to my Flipper dolphins, that's exactly right."

### *Lights, Camera—Showtime!*

The first Flipper movie debuted in 1963, and the TV show followed in 1964. If you've never seen it, you can view clips online.

Want some spoilers behind the illusion? While Flipper is male, all the dolphin performers were female, and Flipper's high-pitched chatter was dubbed by Mel Blanc, the voice actor behind Bugs Bunny, Woody Woodpecker, and other cartoon characters. In the show, Flipper resides in the ocean and chooses to visit the lagoon where the human protagonists live. In reality, Kathy was kept on the set—in a manufactured, two-hundred-square-yard lake—and the other four dolphins were held in small steel tanks.

O'Barry lived on set, too, in the very house where the lead characters reside. "I lived on site for seven years, for seven days a week," O'Barry says.

Each week, the TV script called for some new behavior or trick O'Barry had to teach.

One time he taught Kathy to tailwalk while wearing a hula skirt around her fluke, as if hula dancing.

Another time, he trained Susie to toss a fish into a boat without eating it. O'Barry says, "This was complicated because usually when Susie had a fish in her mouth, it went only one way: down."

The hardest trick was teaching Kathy to swim into an underwater cave. "Dolphins have an instinctive fear of underwater openings, the same as our fear of falling," O'Barry says. It's unclear why, but perhaps when dolphins use echolocation, "the return signals are jumbled in a scary way."

No fish bribe could get Kathy to enter the cave set, so O'Barry practiced swimming in and out with her, while hugging her shaking body, until they were able to get the shot of her swimming alone.

O'Barry was aware of the inherent conflict in his relationship with the dolphins. He was like their jailer, but "I was also their friend. Or I tried to be. To them I was necessarily one of the enemy, but at least a friendly enemy."

"I did what I had to do to get their trust," O'Barry says, since without trust, "there would have been no TV show."

For instance, before transporting Kathy to a new shooting location, they had to catch her in a net, but this made her extremely agitated and afraid—so O'Barry allowed himself to get caught in the same net with her. As both were lifted up, "I would put my arm around her and rub her dorsal fin. I could feel the tension. 'Don't be afraid,' I would say softly. 'I'm here and I'll take care of you.'"

Then each Friday night at 7:30 pm, when the TV show *Flipper* aired, O'Barry positioned a television set at the end of the dock to watch the episode with the dolphins.

"And that's when I knew they were self-aware. I could tell when the dolphins recognized themselves and each other. Kathy, for example, would recognize the shots she was in, Susie would recognize her shots, and so on. Dolphins are hard to read because you have to look at body language."

### *Life in a Bathtub*

A glance from the captive world.
Photo copyright © 2025 maddalenabearzi/OCS (under NOAA permit).

Kathy was young when she first arrived at the aquarium, and "her personality was cooperative, curious, and communicative," O'Barry says.

Over time that changed, "and it was totally different between when the film crew was there and when I was alone with her. Like all captive dolphins, she suffered from extreme depression. I call it Captive Dolphin Depression Syndrome."

The public never sees this because, for one thing, dolphins learn that show-time means mealtime. "They're looking for food, and they know they have to perform to get it. They open their mouths, and to humans, it seems like they're smiling. They're not. It's an illusion."

One of their first adjustments is eating dead fish, which isn't natural. "They're not scavengers," O'Barry says. "But when they get hungry enough, they learn."

The pools where dolphins are kept are, by the measure of the sea, bathtubs, and individual steel tanks are like straightjackets. Worse than the physical stress is "their psychological distortion," O'Barry says. Dolphins have eyes, but sound is their primary sense. They use echolocation to see, and O'Barry wonders, "What must it have seemed like in a steel tank where every shot ricochets crazily back at them like a pool of Babel? I can think only that the tank they were in was to them like a house of mirrors would be to us."

Even sleeping is difficult. Wild dolphins (as well as killer whales) sleep while moving in pods. Their minds are half-awake, so sleeping alone and unmoving causes anxiety. Bobbing in shallow tanks can cause sunburn and dehydration. The unrelieved stress and boredom can also lead to self-harming behaviors and eating disorders that resemble bulimia.

Almost all trainers care for their animals as best as they can, but human standards of care can never meet a dolphin's needs.

Looking back, O'Barry says:

> [The dolphins] were entirely dependent on human beings, swimming with them, playing with them, and receiving endless signals, human imprints overriding nature. And in all that time they hadn't chased a single live fish and gulped it down. Living in tanks they could never get up to full speed for very long in a straight line, they could never dive down and down and feel the pressure building just for the hell of it, nor did they dare let loose a real blast of sonar. Living in isolation for years, their natural dolphin ways were corrupted and distorted, their native memories blurred and forgotten....
>
> And socially they were misfits. They had lost their place in the hierarchy of a pod and had no idea where to go for food, safety, love.... The pod is where a dolphin discovers its own identity.

### *Too Late for Flipper, But Not Others*

When O'Barry got the call, he raced over as fast as he could. It was 1970.

The *Flipper* series ended in 1967, and afterward, O'Barry quit training and moved on to other work. He only rarely visited the Flipper dolphins, who were still at the Miami Seaquarium.

Then the aquarium's supervisor contacted O'Barry to tell him Kathy was in trouble.

She'd been moved to one of the small steel tanks, and she was badly sunburned. "Big ugly black blisters covered almost her whole body," O'Barry says, "and she lay there on the surface of the water, barely moving."

"My God! My God!" he remembers crying. "What have I done?"

O'Barry jumped into the tank, and Kathy slipped into his arms. "She looked me right in the eye, took a breath, held it—and she didn't take another one."

O'Barry tried to open her blowhole. He squeezed her ribcage to start her breathing, "but she was dead and nothing could be done about it. I let her go and she sank to the bottom."

Dolphins (like all cetaceans) don't breathe automatically, the way humans do. To avoid drowning, they can choose when to inhale—once they're at the surface. This also means they can choose *not* to breathe.

For this reason, O'Barry is convinced Kathy deliberately committed suicide by holding her breath till she suffocated.

Kathy was "the dolphin I most dearly loved," O'Barry says, and "when Kathy died in my arms, something of myself died, too."

O'Barry calls this his turning point. Literally overnight, "my goal became to free captive dolphins and put an end to their abuse for human entertainment."

To accomplish that, he founded the Dolphin Project, which for over fifty years has led efforts to release and rehabilitate dolphins all over the world. His efforts to end dolphin hunts in Taiji, Japan, was the focus of the 2009, Oscar-winning documentary *The Cove*.

O'Barry's advice for those who want to help animals is simple: Do what speaks to you. He says:

> There's always ways to help that do not require you to be on the front lines. Public awareness and education are hugely important; you can find your own voice and means to be an effective activist.

—

## Of Singing and Sadness

In Auckland, New Zealand, there once lived a locally famous pig named after a universally famous A. A. Milne character, Piglet. In part, Piglet was beloved for her positive qualities. According to author Jeffrey Moussaieff Masson, she was "immaculate, well-mannered, sensitive, intelligent, and kind to strangers."

More than that, Piglet enjoyed violin music, and "she especially seemed to enjoy music on the beach at night when there was a full moon." She had, Masson says, a "special affinity for music, water, night, and moon" that caused her to vocalize "the sweetest sounds … as if she were actually singing to the moon."

What was going on inside dear Piglet? Masson suggests she may have had "access to feelings humans have not yet known."

### *A Familiar Loss of Feeling*

Pigs display a wide range of emotions, such as joy, anger, fear, curiosity, and playfulness. Like humans, they also become bored when confined, and when isolated for too long, they can experience lethargy, nonresponsiveness, and even learned helplessness.

Researcher Françoise Wemelsfelder studies animal welfare, and she has found that caged animals exhibit the same sorts of behaviors that people do when they are depressed and feel "imprisoned" in their suffering, even if they are not literally imprisoned. Confined animals can engage in repetitive behaviors—called "stereotypic behaviors" or "stereotypies"—that aren't seen in wild animals. These can include continual rocking or pacing, unrelieved scratching or licking, chewing the air, biting the bars of a cage, eating their own feces or vomit, and harming themselves or others.

Might this curious pig sing to the moon?
Photo by Mali Maeder/Pexels.

Animals can also give up.

Wemelsfelder says that pigs "are naturally inquisitive and alert animals. If I enter a pen with young pigs, after a moment's hesitation they quickly approach and vigorously sniff and nibble my hand. But they're also quick to withdraw; one unexpected movement from me and they back away."

This alertness disappears within the sterile, monotonous, restrictive environment of an industrial farm—where pigs are often kept in dirty, dark, cramped, concrete pens with nothing to do except eat and sleep. This can drive out not just joy but all emotion.

"I gained a clear impression of this in a young female pig that had been housed alone for many months in a small barren pen," Wemelsfelder writes.

> She was sitting on the floor, her hind legs stretched underneath her, her back hunched, her head and ears drooping, and her tongue occasionally hanging out of her mouth. She had been sitting this way for quite some time, and my entrance into the pen had little effect. When I sat down next to her and carefully touched her, she glanced at me but didn't move. As the moments passed, I was struck by the soft, gentle, helpless quality of her passivity, the total absence of hostility, fear, or any other active response. She was present only vaguely, her apathy such a stark contrast to what pigs normally are like.

### *Recognizing Quiet Emotions*

Some of our most important emotions are expressed quietly. The emotional state of the pig Wemelsfelder met was defined by withdrawal, by a lack of reaction.

She writes, "Yet the soft quality of a pig's helplessness signals a suffering that is serious rather than slight. It speaks of a loss of communication, of a lost ability to cope. I found the quiet emptiness emanating from the pig poignant and sad."

To know animals better, we have to pay attention to the subtle cues that reveal much. This applies to all emotions, positive and negative.

Jeffrey Masson says that other pigs have been known to sing to the moon. This seems bizarre, but as Masson reminds us, they are nocturnal animals. What might that bright celestial orb inspire in them?

"Several people who live near pigs have told me," he says, "that they have awakened to strange sounds during the night. Sure enough, out their window, they spotted a pig looking up at the full moon, emitting mournful sounds much like singing."

## Get Started: The Problem with Zoos and Waterparks

Knowing that animals can get the blues, we shouldn't be surprised that captivity can cause depression. Among ourselves, imprisonment is a form of punishment because it's painful to be separated from family and community. When children do something wrong, parents sometimes punish them by taking away phones and "grounding" them—thus enforcing isolation.

In fact, lots of research has been done on what's called "captivity effects" in animals. This refers to a range of negative physical and psychological reactions, as described in "Of Singing and Sadness."

We keep animals captive in many contexts, but here we want to focus on zoos and waterparks. In essence, life in a zoo can drive some individuals crazy. Bill Travers, cofounder of the Born Free Foundation, calls this *zoochosis*—or the psychosis of zoo animals.

By their own definition, zoos exist to serve three main purposes: entertainment, education, and conservation. Zoos provide exciting encounters with wild species people normally would never meet, and they strive to educate the public about animals and conservation, while also trying to protect and preserve endangered species.

Experts debate whether zoos succeed at education and conservation in meaningful ways. Some zoos do better than others at educating visitors and conserving some species, but few if any zoo animals are ever returned to nature. The real question is, are the stated goals of zoos and waterparks worth the suffering captivity can cause to individual animals?

This question is particularly important when it comes to charismatic megafauna—those large, intelligent, social mammals who most people want to see: elephants, great apes, rhinos, and lions; dolphins and orcas. These species suffer most when confinement keeps them from expressing their normal behaviors.

Ultimately, no matter how well zoos and waterparks care for their animals, there isn't an enclosure big enough, nor enrichment stimulating enough, to satisfy animals who are smart enough to understand their predicament, who remember and grieve for lost family and a lost society, and who normally range freely across entire landscapes.

### ***If You See Something, Say Something***

When you visit zoos or waterparks, observe animals for yourself. Do they seem content or agitated, happy or sad? Do the cages or enclosures seem adequate? Do animals live alone or with others? From the animals' perspective, is there anything fun to do? Beyond entertainment, does the zoo seem to be fulfilling its mission: Is it educating you? Is it actively involved in wildlife conservation?

Perhaps ask park staff what a day in the zoo is like for the animals.

Then, if something bothers you, speak out. That could be as simple as filling out a visitor response with the zoo. These businesses want happy customers, and if enough customers complain, that can inspire change. The louder we raise our voices—by speaking as part of a group or broadcasting on social media—the more effective our voices can be.

A few years ago, after reading about Happy, an elephant at the Bronx Zoo, a high school student contacted Marc to ask what she could do to shut the zoo down. Of course, she alone couldn't do that, but Marc encouraged her to join others to raise awareness (see "Get Started: Defining Animals—Laws, Regulations, and Rights").

Some zoos and waterparks fail their animals so badly they deserve to be shut down and turned into rescue and rehabilitation facilities. Many also engage in harmful practices that should be ended. These include moving animals among zoos, captive-breeding programs, and killing healthy animals just because there isn't enough space for them or the animals don't fit their breeding program. Zoos often call these "surplus animals"—which is another example of objectifying language—and they sanitize these unnecessary killings by calling it *euthanasia*. But these aren't merciful deaths for animals who are terminally ill or in severe pain, and Marc calls this practice *zoothanasia.*

Ultimately, we may need to accept that certain species only belong in the wild. The problem with zoos, as Caitlin O'Connell says, is that maybe "it's not right for you to be able to see the whole wide world in your backyard."

# 6

# you're no good

## Frustration, Anger, Disgust, and Contempt

Two house cats have a disagreement.
Photo by helen2552/iStock.com.

Anger and disgust are primary emotions like happiness, sadness, and fear. They often appear raw and unfiltered, and so are usually easy to recognize.

Some consider disgust an "evolutionarily primitive" emotion. It's perhaps an instinctual reaction to rotten food that once kept us safe. But moral disgust has also been observed in social animals like chimpanzees.

In fact, anger and frustration are important to recognize. Failure to do so can get us into real trouble, since angry animals sometimes strike back.

—

## Want a Nut

In 1977, researcher Irene Pepperberg decided to study avian minds. She wanted to see if a bird could display the same smarts as chimpanzees, and she chose to work with an African grey parrot she named Alex, "an animal with a brain the size of a shelled walnut, but one that could talk," she says.

Pepperberg got more than she bargained for.

Purchased at a Chicago pet store, Alex turned out to be a brat.

### *Learning to Say No*

Irene Pepperberg and Alex.
Photo courtesy of Irene Pepperberg.

Early on, Alex learned to say "no."

He didn't mimic. He used no when we might expect, by refusing things he didn't want. He loved chewing corks to a nub and immediately asking for a new one by saying, "Cork." Irene once got tired of this game and handed him a chewed remnant. Alex shot back, "No! Cork!"

He also used no defiantly "to express his unwillingness to go along with a training session," Pepperberg says. "It was amusing, unless you happened to be the trainer trying to get some work done."

As Pepperberg taught him words and confirmed his comprehension, Alex sometimes said no to every question.

Slowly, they made progress. Alex learned to identify colors, shapes, and amounts, so Pepperberg kept raising the bar. Could Alex generalize colors and shapes to correctly identify new objects he hadn't seen before?

He could, but to prove Alex understood with scientific rigor, Pepperberg repeated tests dozens and dozens of times in multiple ways. But think about it: How might you feel if, for weeks on end, you were asked to solve "2 + 2 = X"? That's right, Alex got bored and started misbehaving. He'd disrupt objects on a tray, bite the tray, preen, and turn his backside to Pepperberg, "a gesture too obvious to need translation."

Over time, Pepperberg says, Alex would "show his opinion of the boring task at hand by playing with our heads." If she asked, "What color key?" he would name every color except the right one. "Eventually, he became quite ingenious with this game, having more fun getting us agitated rather than giving us the answers we wanted and he surely knew."

Call it annoyance, petulance, frustration, aggravation, irritation, discontent, or even mockery, Alex's feelings were clear.

Pepperberg says, "He was like the bright little kid at school who finds none of the work challenging and so passes the time by making trouble."

### Answering the Question

Alex's stubbornness occasionally triggered stunning breakthroughs. An impatient student, he'd jump ahead and reveal capabilities Pepperberg hadn't thought to test for.

Presented with an apple, a fruit he'd never seen, Alex called it a "banerry," a word he'd never used. This drove Pepperberg nuts. She was trying to teach the word "apple," but Alex kept insisting on "banerry." Then a linguist friend suggested Alex might have put together two words to make a single new word, which is called lexical elision. Alex already knew the words *banana* and *cherry*, and since an apple combined both, being red outside and sweet inside, he might have made up his own word for this fruit. Pepperberg says, "It really did look like some bird brain creativity of a sort never previously seen."

Another time, Alex refused to cooperate for two entire weeks during some number trials. He'd look away, preen, respond with colors or shapes, or deliberately say the wrong number. Trying to turn the tables, Pepperberg finally asked for something that wasn't on the tray, a group of five things: "What color five?"

"None," Alex said instantly.

Alex knew the word *none*, but he'd never used it in a way that reflected the concept of zero, or "the absence of existence." Pepperberg wasn't sure what to think. Animals aren't supposed to understand that.

Then there was the time Pepperberg was teaching Alex phonemes, or the separate, individual sounds that combine to make a complete word. She wasn't trying to teach him to read. Rather, without being able to read, could he recognize individual letters and understand how they combined into words?

One day, after Alex had already shown he could sound out letters, Pepperberg was testing him again in front of observers. In typical Alex fashion, he became disruptive.

Each time he answered a question correctly, by identifying a letter sound—like "sss" for S—he said, "Want a nut."

Pepperberg refused. Alex would eat nuts all day if she let him. So, she kept asking more phoneme questions.

Then this happened:

> "Alex, wait," I said. "What color is 'or'?"
>
> "Orange."
>
> "Good bird!"
>
> "Want a nut." Alex was obviously getting more than a little frustrated. He finally got very slitty-eyed, always a sign he was up to something. He looked at me and said slowly, "Want a nut. Nnn … uh … tuh."

> I was stunned. It was as if he were saying, *Hey, stupid, do I have to spell it out for you?*

In an instant, Alex had jumped far ahead in their training, skipping past letter sounds to sounding out whole words.

Pepperberg wonders, "Perhaps he was really saying to us, *I know where you're headed with this work! Let's get on with it.*"

Pepperberg summarizes Alex's emotional complexity:

> The media portrayed Alex as a brainiac, and he was—a bird brainiac. But there were many more sides to Mr. A. than just his cognitive achievements. He was bossy and obstinate. He was playful, not just with toys but intellectually, when he deliberately gave wrong answers. He was mischievous and affectionate. And ... he was supremely confident in who he was as an individual....
>
> Alex taught us how little we know about animal minds and how much more there is to discover.

—

## On Trial: The People Vs. Octopuses

When evaluating whether human-octopus interactions rise to the level of punishable crimes (whether misdemeanors or felonies), it's important to review previous lawsuits and established case law.*

Below are three legal case briefs that summarize lawsuits that have come before courts in various jurisdictions. As the results show, despite findings of injury in several cases, extenuating circumstances invariably led octopuses to being let off the hook.

In summary: Don't piss off octopuses, who seem emboldened by the ongoing lack of administrative justice.

**Case Brief: Aquarium Staff Vs. Octopuses**

**Parties:** This class-action lawsuit included plaintiffs from several US states and New Zealand. Defendants were octopuses as a species, but mainly giant Pacific octopuses.

**Determinative Facts:**

- A night biologist at the Seattle Aquarium claimed multiple unprovoked attacks with jets of water by an unnamed octopus. Defense argued that beaming a bright flashlight into tank prompted the angry octopus to retaliate.
- An aquarium worker was doused by an octopus during a routine feeding. Defense alleged that, prior to dousing, a conflict had ensued about the client's need to remain in the tank. To keep the octopus from exiting said tank, the worker had doused client with freshwater, and the enraged client responded in kind.
- Multiple labs claimed octopuses regularly and deliberately used jets of water to break lightbulbs or short-circuit lights. A lab in New Zealand claimed fixing damage became so expensive that the octopuses had to be returned to the sea.

**Issue:** Are octopuses liable for dry cleaning bills and property damage, as well as emotional distress of targeted humans?

**Ruling:** Suit was deemed frivolous and tossed out.

**Reasoning:** No personal injuries resulted from either dowsings or broken bulbs. Further, extenuating circumstances showed octopuses had cause to be angry. It is well-known that octopuses cannot tolerate freshwater, making aquarium staff liable for causing distress. Further, octopuses hate bright lights, making institutions responsible for maintaining appropriate light levels.

Going forward, the court encouraged appropriate raingear when working near octopus tanks. Further, the court reminded plaintiffs that octopuses can only pay in shells, making remuneration doubtful even if the ruling was in their favor.

**Case Brief: Peter Dews Vs. Charles**

| | |
|---|---|
| **Parties:** | Plaintiff was Harvard scientist Peter Dews. Defendant was Charles, an octopus. |
| **Determinative Facts:** | • During a research experiment to teach three octopuses to pull a lever to release food, two octopuses, Albert and Bertram, completed all tasks, while Charles did not cooperate and destroyed equipment, thus "leading to a premature termination of the experiment," Dews alleged.<br>• Dews claimed, "Charles had a high tendency to direct jets of water out of the tank; specifically, they were in the direction of the experimenter."<br>• Charles repeatedly used tentacles to grab the lamp and pull the bulb into the water, thus ruining it. This behavior was, Dews said, "obviously incompatible with lever-pulling."<br>• "Whereas Albert and Bertram gently operated the lever," Dews explained that Charles "applied great force," so much so that the lever bent and broke. |
| **Issue:** | Is Charles liable for damaged property, ruining of an experiment, harming Dews's professional reputation, and injuring scientific inquiry? |
| **Ruling:** | Were Charles a person, he would have been charged with felony property damage and misdemeanor loss of reputation. Not being a "person" as defined by human law, Charles's case did not belong in a human court. Dews was referred to an octopus court, should he find one. |
| **Reasoning:** | Charles's property destruction was willful and significant, and his contemptuous disregard for Dews and his work led to snickering by scientific peers. However, seen in a different light, Charles's angry reaction might be considered relevant to the experiment. In general, octopuses are too smart to play along with boring, repetitive tasks, leading the court to question the relative intelligence of Albert and Bertram. |

**Case Brief: Jean Boal Vs. an Octopus**

| | |
|---|---|
| **Parties:** | Plaintiff was University of Pennsylvania cephalopod researcher Jean Boal. Defendant was a female octopus, unnamed. |
| **Determinative Facts:** | • Boal was performing the routine task of feeding the lab's octopuses along a row of tanks, giving each pieces of thawed squid.<br>• After feeding them all, Boal noticed the octopus in the first tank seemed to be waiting for her. The octopus was holding the squid in, according to prosecutors, "a conspicuous and vaguely threatening manner."<br>• After making eye contact with Boal, and continuing to watch her the whole time, the octopus traversed to the tank's outflow pipe and propelled the squid down the drain. |
| **Issue:** | Is the octopus guilty of littering? |
| **Ruling:** | Since evidence of the squid was lost, defendant was found not guilty. |
| **Reasoning:** | Upon cross-examination, Boal admitted that the lab's thawed squid wasn't always the freshest, though she protested that it was never rotten. She also complained that octopuses are picky eaters. However, the court determined the octopus may have acted in self-defense. Further, Boal admitted the tank was missing a dedicated trash receptacle, so the octopus lacked other options for disposal. In the octopus's, er, shoes, the court suggested they would have been disgusted, too. |

* *Authors' Note:* These trials and case briefs are not real, but the octopuses are and the events are true. Most importantly, like all animals, octopuses have no rights (see "Get Started: Defining Animals—Laws, Regulations, and Rights"). Not only can't animals be charged with crimes, they have no legal standing or recourse for harm done to them. Silly as it is, this "thought experiment" raises an important question: If captive animals could advocate for themselves, what "crimes" might they charge us with and what might they ask for?

## The Inner Lives of Plants

Do plants "cry" when injured? Do they "lie" to bees? Do they call for wasp mercenaries when being eaten by caterpillars? Do they respond to music?

Plants don't have brains like animals, but maybe they don't need them. Researchers are finding that plants act in ways that, were they animals, we'd consider intelligent and sentient. As unbelievable as it sounds, researchers have observed plant behaviors that resemble emotions, learning, memory, agency, individualized personalities, and even social lives.

For instance, researchers have found that when plants need water or have had their stems cut, they make "airborne sounds" that are too high-pitched for us to hear. "It is a bit like popcorn—very short clicks," a researcher said. "It is not singing."

Evening primroses have been found to produce sweeter nectar when they hear flying bees, and different tones cause broccoli to produce more antioxidants and alfalfa sprouts to make more vitamin C.

When caterpillars eat corn, the plant senses their saliva and releases a compound that attracts a specific parasitic wasp. The wasp injects their larva inside the caterpillar, and when the larvae hatch, they eat the caterpillar and use its husk for their cocoons. Plant researcher Zoë Schlanger says, "You can think of that as a plant using a tool."

Meanwhile, yellow monkey flowers trick bees into pollinating them even though they don't produce much or any pollen. Why bother when they can produce a chemical that signals to bees that they have lots of pollen? The bees arrive, pollinate the plant, and fly away empty-handed (or empty-legged).

Bean plants seem to show flexible, directed behavior as they search for a pole to climb. When they find one, they "lunge"—in slow motion—as their electrical activity spikes ... almost as if they are excited.

Whatever is going on inside plants, it is so alien to animal biology that scientists don't know how to understand it or what to call it. But Schlanger says, "What matters is watching what they actually do. And what they do is make decisions in real time and plan for the future."

Marc thinks this important research might change our notions of sentience. In fact, the current debates over plant sentience mirror the debates over animal sentience from thirty or forty years ago, and research might lead to the same conclusions. He says, "As the evidence piles up, the debate is less about *if* plants are smart and emotional, but rather *how* they experience the world and *why* these capacities have evolved."

## Don't Diss the Matriarch

"Freya was refusing to follow any of the signals I had taught her."

A seven-thousand-pound killer whale, Freya was the dominant matriarch among the captive orcas at Marineland in Antibes, France, and her trainer, John Hargrove, had just entered her pool to start a training session.

Almost immediately, Freya herded Hargrove into the center of the pool—ignoring his commands and the fish reward in his hand.

Sensing trouble, Hargrove dropped the fish and tried to avoid Freya, but he says, she "countered every move I made like a skilled soccer player—and I became the ball she was so nimbly positioning in her game."

Freya dove briefly and resurfaced, Hargrove says, "slowly and deliberately, turning sideways to make contact with the left side of my body." She slid along Hargrove and stopped once her tail flukes were next to him, the right submerged, the left in the air, "just a foot or two away from my head."

Hargrove wondered:

> Was she going to strike me in the face? If she did, the force and weight could easily break my neck and kill me. But she decided to tease me some more, swirling around to face me, her blue eyes bulging, wide and strained.

Around the pool, the other trainers sounded the emergency recall tone. This signaled the orcas to stop whatever they were doing and go to the pool's edge. Freya ignored it, and Hargrove recognized all the "signs of an oncoming episode of aggression": The blue irises of her upset eyes were surrounded with red veins. The muscles of her back were tight. And she was emitting telltale vocalizations.

"I knew what was coming," Hargrove says, as Freya submerged and positioned her mouth beneath him.

He told the other trainers to call the paramedics.

### *The Peaceful Nature of Killer Whales*

Killer whales, also known as orcas, are the largest species of dolphin. They are, according to ecologist Carl Safina, "intelligent, maternal, long-lived, cooperative, intensely social, devoted to family," and though similar to humans in many ways, "notably less violent."

Further, Safina claims that "no free-living killer whale has ever killed a human." They eat everything else as prey, even whales, but not us.

This isn't for lack of chances. They never capsize boats, overturn kayaks, snack on swimmers, or grab people from the beach, the way they do with seals. Deepening the mystery, orcas, like all dolphins, have a history of helping people, particularly guiding the boats of researchers when they get lost in fog.

Lack of aggression is a defining characteristic of their complex, matriarchal society. Safina says, "The basic social unit is a family led by a senior female matriarch, with her children and her daughters' children." Even male killer whales stay with their birth family; they leave for short periods to mate but then return. Children stay with their mother till she dies.

Individuals can have conflicts—usually among orcas from different populations and related to territory—but killer whales typically resolve issues among themselves without violence.

Trained killer whales perform at SeaWorld in San Diego, California, 2010.
Photo by Egon Bömsch, imageBROKER.com/Alamy.

### *A Disordered Community and "Warped Psychologies"*

Captivity, however, changes orcas. It subverts their society and leads to what, compared to wild orcas, has been called "abnormal" behavior.

Similar to captive dolphins, orcas suffer a litany of physical and psychological problems due to confinement, lack of proper exercise, altered diet, isolation, and boredom. Even the chemical-laced water is different.

Hargrove says training and performances provide killer whales with "a temporary escape," but afterward, the animals "go right back to their shell of an existence, floating motionless in the pools, dealing with the monotony of captive life, bored out of their minds.... It is the kind of ennui that can be fatal—to both whale and human."

Captive orcas try to reestablish a social order among themselves, but this is nearly impossible in sea-life parks, which combine orcas from around the globe. This is like gathering people from foreign countries. Killer whale populations have "distinct dialects," Hargrove says, and the inability to communicate clearly is one theory for why orcas are so violent in captivity: Physical domination becomes the easiest way to establish a hierarchy.

In a way virtually unseen in the wild, there is "a reign of terror imposed by dominant females" in sea-life parks, according to Hargrove.

This is embodied by raking, or being "scratched or cut deeply by a whale's teeth, like the wounds that might be inflicted on flesh by a rake," Hargrove says. Sometimes wounds are superficial, but severe cuts can be "ugly and bloody."

Raking is rare among wild orcas. It's discouraged by matriarchs and mainly used to warn misbehaving young calves.

In sea-life parks, orcas know that defying the matriarch risks being raked. If the dominant female refuses to participate in training, neither will any other killer whale.

Taken together, the impacts of captivity mean that killer whales, Hargrove says, "are no longer really orcas but mutants, genetically killer whales but made up of warped psychologies."

### Getting the Message

Freya mouthed Hargrove around his waist. "My body was in her jaws," Hargrove says, "like a twig in a dog's mouth, one that could snap with just the wrong amount of pressure."

Freya pulled him underwater and released him without biting. When Hargrove resurfaced, she did it again.

He'd seen this pattern with other trainers who'd been threatened. Hargrove says, "She might come back to drag me under again and again until I became unconscious in the water from the repeated dunking."

Then, at last, Freya responded to the emergency tone, went to the pool's lip, and was rewarded with fish for obeying. But she was still watching Hargrove. He knew if he tried to swim away, she'd become furious, and "she might no longer toy with me," Hargrove says. "I chose to gamble."

Hargrove understood he'd done something wrong. Freya was letting him know she was mad at him. So he decided to engage with her while she was feeling rewarded. He told the other trainers to send Freya back to him in the middle of the pool.

When she arrived, Hargrove asked her to perform a few simple behaviors, which she did, and then he asked for a "pec-push," which is essentially giving a trainer a ride while they hang on to the orca's lower jaw.

She did this, too, and when Hargrove reached the rim of the pool, he hopped out and gave Freya an entire bucket's worth of fish "to reward her for cooperating, for letting me go."

Hargrove says his knees were shaking. It was "the first and only time in my career I was truly unnerved by killer whale aggression."

But *why* was Freya mad?

Afterward, Hargrove figured it out. Just before, he'd been training alone with her son, Val, in the adjacent pool. "I noticed that Freya was watching us intently from her pool," Hargrove says, and she must have been "nursing a grievance. She did not like the fact that Val was receiving so much attention while she was stewing behind her gate. She was the dominant whale, after all."

Thinking back, he remembered Freya displacing Val when they practiced together—swimming ahead of him, acting jealous, and seeking preferential treatment from the trainers. She was easily slighted and always reminded others—orcas and humans—of her rank.

Message received.

After that, Hargrove says, he and Freya "figured out how to work with each other." And they did for several years, till Hargrove left the park.

Hargrove concludes:

> You might say I trained her. But that would be generous. More accurately, she had made certain I learned the right way to treat her. Once that was established, the monster would become an angel to me. But now I know: monster and angel can be one and the same.

## Get Started: Defining Animals—Laws, Regulations, and Rights

How we define animals guides our relationship with them. It expresses who we think they are and what standards of care we consider ethical. In theory, our definition of animals should be the basis for our animal laws and regulations.

But is it? How *do* we, as a society, define nonhuman animals?

In fact, there is no single, mutually agreed-upon definition. Our rules change by animal and sometimes by context. Defining animals generates lots of controversy, especially recently as research has exploded our understanding of their inner lives. Once regarded as emotionless beings controlled by instinct, most nonhuman animals are now considered, to one degree or another, conscious, emotional, thinking beings who are constantly making decisions.

This is increasingly putting society in an uncomfortable place.

Consider dogs.

Our often-beloved canine companions are frequently regarded like four-legged humans. We know they live in their own scent-driven world, but that difference hardly matters: We accept that dogs love and grieve, scheme and play; that they can save our lives and learn our language.

Yet as smart and emotional as dogs are, they are legally considered property. While there are regulations against extreme cruelty, we can buy, sell, keep, and dispose of dogs like a car or sweater. The same is true for every other animal in the world. Even wild animals are legally treated like human property. In a court of law, not a single animal enjoys an inherent right to life except ourselves.

Human convenience, not our definitions of animals, is what usually guides laws.

One of the most egregious examples is the US Federal Animal Welfare Act (AWA). This governs standards of animal care in agriculture, industry, and scientific research. But in 2004, this was changed to redefine the term *animal* so that it excludes laboratory-bred rats and mice. That's right, even though rats and mice are obviously animals, the AWA says those born in labs are not. Why? Because rats and mice are the main animals used in scientific research, and if they qualified for protection under the AWA, most of that research would have to stop.

The AWA also exempts most farm animals, and the Humane Slaughter Act exempts chickens and fish. Thus, despite our definitions of animals, our laws get carved with loopholes that allow animal abuse if it suits the needs of business and society.

### *Welfare Versus Well-Being*

Today, many people are trying to revise laws and regulations around the world using two main concepts: animal welfare and animal well-being. Animal welfare focuses on improving how animals are treated within their current situations so that they experience the "five freedoms."

These are

1. freedom from hunger or thirst;
2. freedom from discomfort;
3. freedom from pain, injury, or disease;
4. freedom to express normal behaviors; and
5. freedom from fear and distress.

These are laudable, important goals, but in practice, animal welfare efforts are often inadequate. They focus on things like bigger cages and replacing certain harmful practices (like declawing, dehorning, and debeaking) while leaving cages themselves and systems intact. When successful, these efforts make animals somewhat more comfortable, but the basic harsh conditions remain.

We promote animal well-being. This focuses on the quality of life of each *individual* animal and promotes much higher standards of care that avoid all forms of abuse. Applying the standards of animal well-being would force major changes in every situation in which animals are used.

### *Animal Rights: Defining Personhood*

Then there are nonhuman animal rights. These seek to redefine a few of the most-intelligent species—such as elephants, great apes, dolphins, and dogs—as "persons" under the law. This status would bestow these species with inherent rights to liberty, autonomy, equality, and fairness. Founded by the indefatigable attorney Steve Wise—who passed away in 2024—the Nonhuman Rights Project (NhRP) is leading this effort. They propose that "the law has to catch up to what we know about nonhuman animals, and courts and legislatures have to begin figuring out which species are entitled to which rights on what basis."

One of NhRP's most famous cases involved Happy, an elephant at the Bronx Zoo. Happy was the first elephant to pass the so-called mirror test demonstrating self-awareness. Yet for four decades, what she has communicated most has been her unhappiness at being kept alone in a bare, one-acre enclosure. In 2018, the NhRP decided to legally represent Happy by submitting a writ of *habeas corpus*. While the legal approach of this case was complex and unique—it had never been tried with nonhuman animals before—the upshot is that *habeas corpus* allows a person to challenge their own captivity, and so they are brought before a judge to determine if their detention is legal. Using this, NhRP appeared before the Bronx Supreme Court. With the support of elephant experts like Cynthia Moss and Joyce Poole, they argued that Happy possesses all the attributes of personhood that define humans: consciousness, a sense of self, the ability to reason, autonomy, and complex emotions.

The NhRP lost its case, and Happy has remained at the Bronx Zoo. If she'd won, she would have been moved to a sanctuary, since she can no longer survive on her own in the wild.

But two of the seven judges dissented, saying that Happy should be considered a legal person. One wrote that Happy "is an intelligent, autonomous being who should be treated with respect and dignity, and who may be entitled to liberty."

One day, as laws catch up with what we know, elephants might be considered legal persons, meaning they couldn't be held in zoos. The AWA might define laboratory-born rats as animals and disallow abusive research. With good reason, people wonder if this will become a "slippery slope." What will happen if we start granting some rights to some animals? What rights? Which animals? Who gets to say?

One day, will we have to let all the dogs run free?

This is where you, the reader of this book, come in. You will decide that future as you consider and perhaps rewrite the laws as we try to align what we know about animals with how, as a society, we care for them.

# 7

# i hung my head

## Pride, Jealousy, Guilt, and Shame

Lakota, the omega or lowest-ranking wolf, crouches down and licks the snout of Kamots, the alpha or top wolf, as a way to acknowledge their hierarchy in the Sawtooth wolf pack, Sawtooth Mountains, Idaho. Photo courtesy of Jim and Jamie Dutcher, founders of Livingwithwolves.org.

Pride, envy, jealousy, embarrassment, guilt, and shame are often called "social emotions." They relate to relationships, living in community, and concern for social status.

These are very familiar feelings. Every collection of humans is concerned with group dynamics. Every person wants to look good and be admired while avoiding blame and shame. The opinions of others matter, and this can lead to lots of deception, trickery, and flattery to get what we want.

Numerous social mammals display these emotions. Chimpanzees, for instance, are known for what Frans de Waal calls a "bipedal swagger," when alpha males stride like Western gunslingers, exuding macho pride. Chimps also exhibit the inward, shrinking posture of shame.

Yet social emotions can be hard to identify correctly. We have a limited understanding of the social lives of nonhuman animals, so we can't always be sure if what looks like envy or shame really is those things.

Whether dogs feel guilty after, say, peeing inside the house has generated lots of debate. A dog's cowed head and worried eyes seem to shout "guilty!"—but maybe not. If a dog doesn't understand that peeing is "wrong," their demeanor might only reflect an expectation of punishment, since their person is yelling at them about *something*.

Doggie pride is another matter. Marc once asked an audience of fifty people if they thought their dogs "showed off." Everyone said yes, and a few said their cats did, too. Their animals loved to flaunt a treasured object so everyone could see. Marc has recorded the same behavior in wild coyotes, who will parade a juicy bone as if taunting others to take it.

When we observe these emotions, one important thing they tell us is that animals know and care that others are watching.

—

## Field Notes: Penguin Pranksters

*Here, Marc describes some of his adventures doing fieldwork:*

Fieldwork is extremely varied and always interesting. Sometimes it entails sitting back and watching, and sometimes it involves indirect or direct interactions with animals. When my students and I studied coyotes living in Grand Teton National Park, we sat on Blacktail Butte near Moose, Wyoming, for hours on end using high-powered spotting scopes and binoculars to observe individuals. But just as often we tracked coyotes on foot, snowshoes, or skis in the cold and dismal dead of winter until we, but not they, were exhausted. Fieldwork is not for the squeamish or faint of heart.

Marc pretending to be a penguin at the research field site, Ross Island, Antarctica, 1975.

I once had the distinct pleasure of collecting elephant dung with George Wittemyer at the Samburu National Reserve in northern Kenya. Perhaps only an ethologist would respond to the offer, "Hey, you want to help me collect elephant dung?" with an excited yes. I jumped at the opportunity.

A few days before we went dung collecting, I was sitting in a truck with renowned elephant researcher Iain Douglas-Hamilton when a six-year-old female elephant ran toward me, stopped just short of the door, whacked the front of the truck with her trunk, and casually walked away. Then a few hours later, Hewa, a large female elephant, sauntered up to the research vehicle, looked at me as if to say, *Who do you think you are?*, and passed wind about two feet from my face.

After Hewa's warm welcome, I turned to Iain and asked, "What's happening?"

"Oh, they're just showing you who's boss in a nice way," he said.

Years ago, I also had the unique opportunity to study Adélie penguins at the Cape Crozier penguin rookery on Ross Island, Antarctica. When we once took a helicopter to the rookery from the McMurdo Station base, the helicopter's ground speed was 90 knots (about a hundred miles per hour), but its air speed was zero knots because of the severe headwinds.

It was Antarctic summer with around eighteen hours of sunlight and temperatures ranging from twenty to thirty degrees Fahrenheit. An average day in the field could easily last fifteen hours. We had to carry all the food, water, and clothes we would need for the day, plus more if bad weather rolled in and we got stuck through the evening. At the site, three other researchers and I shared an eight-by-sixteen-foot hut with no running water or electricity and an outhouse—which we jokingly called the honey bucket—that worked most of the time. Despite the difficulties, it was a wonderful experience I'll never forget.

The first thing I learned was that these small and unbelievably strong, hearty birds don't all look the same. Over time, we could identify individuals by different patterns of black-and-white plumage, by scars, and by their waddle. We also recognized distinct personalities. Some penguins are bold, some shy, and some are frankly obnoxious individuals who continually make a nuisance of themselves. Penguins are survivors. I watched them leaping out of the Ross Sea almost totally eviscerated by leopard seals or killer whales. A few survived for weeks after they were mauled, running around as if nothing had happened.

Penguins also love to play. They would sail down a sheet of ice we called the "penguin highway" and plunge into the Ross Sea as if they were on sleds. Numerous times penguins would sail down the highway, jump in the water, waddle back to the top, and do it again. I wasn't there to study play, but I couldn't help but wonder if the penguins were simply enjoying themselves. There was no obvious reason to do it, so maybe what looked like fun really was fun.

Adélie penguins build nests made of stones. Since stones are in short supply, penguins do what any parent might—steal from other nests. I was very amused by their various stone-stealing strategies. These ranged from brazenly running in at full speed and scooping a stone in their bill to hanging around another penguin's nest as if they didn't have a care in the world. Then when the other penguins were preoccupied, they'd run in and steal a stone. They also changed tactics depending on what the other penguins were doing—were they looking at the would-be thief or preoccupied with their chicks or focused on another interloper?

Because of the countless hours I spent watching these ingenious birds, I got to know a few penguins up close and personally. I can't say exactly what they were feeling as they stole stones, but it often looked like some combination of greed, envy, and jealousy. Clearly, they were scheming and strategizing as they assessed the situation and adapted accordingly. During our arduous days in the field, watching these sitcom-worthy episodes of stone stealing provided wonderful comic relief.

## No Quid Pro Quo

Conservationist Benjamin B. Beck was once conducting an experiment on cooperation using a family of hamadryas baboons at Chicago's Brookfield Zoo. While the experiment showed that baboons will cooperate to achieve a common goal, it also showed how, when fairness is undermined by greed, baboons respond with jealousy, resentment, and deceit.

Just like us.

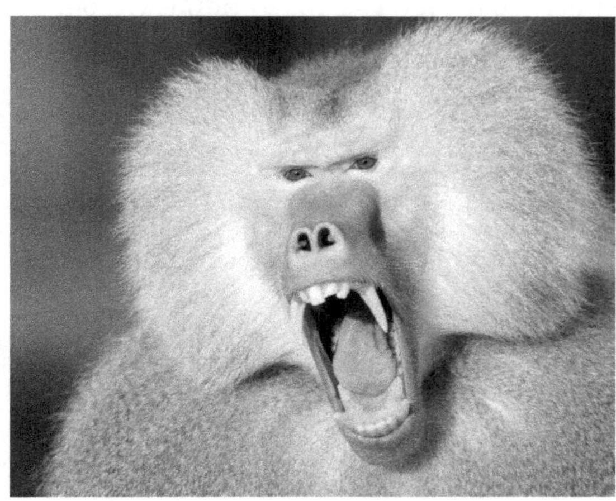

A male hamadryas baboon bares his fangs.
Photo by Andyworks/iStock.com.

Peewee was the dominant male, and researchers taught him to use a long rod to get preferred food that was placed beyond his reach in front of his cage. Peewee lived separately from several family members, whose cage was connected to Peewee's by a door. The catch was, the door was too small for Peewee to pass through, but it was big enough for the other baboons to enter Peewee's cage.

Then researchers put the long rod in the family's cage to see what would happen.

Bedlam, naturally. During four trials, Peewee reached his arm into the family cage, trying to grab the long rod and causing the other baboons to resist and scream. Each time, Peewee was eventually able to nab the rod and use it to get the food—eating most of it and leaving a few unwanted scraps for the others.

On the fifth trial, though, Pat, Peewee's younger sister, got an idea. She immediately picked up the rod and brought it directly to Peewee. This time, Beck says, "There was no snatching (even when the tool was in reach of his cage), no screaming, and no resistance. He used the rod to get the food, and he and Pat each ate about half of it."

That's almost a textbook example of a quid pro quo: a favor for a favor. The researchers continued the experiment to see if things would remain fair.

They did not. Ben says:

> Pat and Peewee quickly refined their cooperative relationship, but her share of the food dwindled. Soon she was getting only about 15 percent. Sometimes she sat next to Peewee as he ate, staring into his face from inches away. Sometimes she simply paced agitatedly around the cage as he dined on his outsized share. Sometimes she surreptitiously placed her hand over a scattered tidbit without looking at it and ate it later when Peewee was distracted. But because of male dominance, she never dared take a choice bit directly, so she got mostly leftovers.

To Ben, Pat was clearly displaying resentment, but she "could not express outright anger or aggression toward a male baboon who was twice her size, had dagger-like canines, and was clearly dominant."

Then something unexpected happened. One day, while Peewee was eating and Pat was circling in frustration, she passed by the cage door and was startled when another baboon poked their head through. "Pat screamed involuntarily," Ben says, and "Peewee leaped to the door, threw Pat out of the way, and began threatening the baboons in the other cage. By chance, however, Pat had landed in the middle of the food pile, and she quickly stuffed her cheek pouches."

No dummy, Pat quickly figured out how to even the score with dominant Peewee. Ben says:

> On their very next cooperative venture, after Pat had brought the tool and Peewee had used it to get and monopolize the food, she went directly to the door between the cages and screamed. There was no other group member on the other side, but again Peewee leaped to the door, pushing Pat aside. She ran directly to the food and again stuffed her pouches.
>
> This maneuver was repeated two or three times before Peewee invented a counterstrategy: He would pull the food pile across the cage floor in his encircling

arms and then sit in the door while he ate. Pat's successful but short-lived strategy for dealing with her resentment of Peewee was foiled.

And thus it remained. Peewee returned to sharing about 15 percent of the food with Pat, which was more than she would have gotten if she didn't help, but nowhere close to the half portion she'd first received … and which she obviously felt she deserved.

### Childhood Inspiration: Leilani Münter

Leilani Münter's motto is "Never underestimate a vegan hippie chick with a race car." For years, Leilani was a professional race car driver, and she remains an animal and environmental activist who, among other honors, is an ambassador for Ric O'Barry's Dolphin Project.

> I have a vivid memory from my elementary school days in Minnesota. I was in first or second grade, and the class was outside on the playground. I was standing by the swing sets, and one of the boys from my class started kicking the ant hills, destroying them seemingly out of boredom and cruelty. I remember being furious and screaming at him, "How would you like it if someone came to your house and destroyed it for no reason?!" I remember being extremely upset about his disregard for other creatures and how it took him mere seconds to destroy the home these tiny creatures had spent days building.
>
> As I grew older, I earned a degree in biology specializing in ecology, behavior, and evolution. After college, I became a professional race car driver. I featured several animal rights documentaries on my race car, including *The Cove* and *Blackfish*, and drove several vegan-themed race cars. We gave away over thirty thousand vegan cheeseburgers to race fans at my races. I sit on the board of two environmental nonprofits and spent several years working with the Oceanic Preservation Society on their film *Racing Extinction*, about the sixth mass extinction of species.
>
> It's funny to think all of this may have been kick started on that playground watching the ant hills. Never believe you are too small to make a difference!

## Sorry Is the Hardest Word

Sometimes siblings can drive us crazy, and figuring out how to live together isn't easy.

Just ask Kanzi and Panbanisha.

These two famous bonobos were half-siblings born five years apart. In the 1980s and 1990s, both participated in groundbreaking research exploring the linguistic abilities of apes. In these studies, lead researcher Dr. Sue Savage-Rumbaugh pioneered the use of computers and lexigrams (symbols that represent words) to teach apes how to communicate with us. Their star pupils, Kanzi and Panbanisha, amazed the world with how smart they were (Panbanisha died in 2012, and Kanzi died in 2025).

These bonobos, our closest relatives, also showed that humans aren't the only species who experience sibling rivalry.

### *A Diva Is Born*

Sue said, "Kanzi could use a keyboard, blow up balloons, solve complicated mazes and puzzles on a computer with a joystick, make stone tools, and understand really difficult sentences."

One time in the woods, Kanzi touched the lexigrams for "marshmallows" and "fire." So, Sue gave him marshmallows and matches and watched as he broke up twigs, lit them with the match, and toasted marshmallows on a stick. Kanzi learned how to play Pac-Man and Minecraft, and in 2024, he defeated the Ender Dragon with the help of another bonobo. Kanzi learned over 350 lexigrams and around three thousand human words. By the time Panbanisha was born in 1985, Kanzi was being filmed regularly for documentaries and TV shows.

Kanzi could also be a pain in the butt. Like the African grey parrot Alex, if Kanzi lost interest or didn't want to participate, he might play dumb or become contrary, "often doing the exact opposite" of whatever Sue asked.

According to Sue, "He had stage presence and charisma. And he loved to play to the camera." But all the attention could get to his head. "When he awoke one morning after a two-week filming session to find the crew had gone, he was so upset that he refused to leave his bedroom. If there was no one to applaud his accomplishments, why bother?"

### *Sharing the Limelight*

Enter Panbanisha. Even as an infant, she showed an amazing understanding of lexigrams and human language, and she became another favorite of researchers and film crews. But Kanzi didn't exactly celebrate his half-sister's success.

Sue said Kanzi became "very jealous of anything Panbanisha did well or got compliments for. When she tried to make stone tools, he bristled." One time, right when Panbanisha was about to hit the rocks perfectly to make a tool, he rushed at her in a ritualized threat display, and Panbanisha dropped the stones. When Panbanisha was writing lexigrams "clearly on the floor—better than he could—he scattered her crayons."

No one likes to be upstaged, particularly by their baby sister. But Panbanisha chose to keep the peace.

"The next time Panbanisha started to make a tool," Sue said, "she just hit the rocks lightly together and looked at Kanzi with an appealingly pitiable 'I can't do it' expression. His male superiority thus affirmed, Kanzi gracefully deigned to make a tool for her and hand it over. Panbanisha was shrewd enough not only to make a tool but to know when it was better not to make a tool and to feign incompetence, allowing her brother to share the fruits of his labor while maintaining his self-image."

Bonobos display tremendous emotional intelligence. Panbanisha deferred to Kanzi so he'd feel better, all in the spirit of living together.

Perhaps Panbanisha could afford to be generous. She was, in fact, better at many of the challenges researchers gave them. She became better at making tools, better at learning to play an electric guitar, and had better language comprehension. By the time Panbanisha died, it was estimated that she knew twice as many human words as Kanzi.

One time, Kanzi was left indoors while Panbanisha was taken outside to learn without being interrupted. Sue said:

> Kanzi screamed and pleaded to go, but we ignored him. Finally, in a fit of pique, he grabbed a toy panda bear and tore off its arms. Then he felt ashamed and tried to put them back. When he couldn't, he carried them around and around the room, keeping his head down and not looking anyone in the eye.

We've all been there—gotten mad, thrown a fit, and then felt sorry. Kanzi knew he'd misbehaved. Perhaps he even recognized that his jealousy was selfish. After all, Kanzi loved his sister.

Sue said, "Kanzi is pure feeling, all feeling, straight from the heart, and the expression of those feelings—jealousy among them—is strong and unadulterated every time."

—

## Get Started: Putting Out the Welcome Mat—Wildlife in Our Backyards

Maybe it's not out of envy or jealousy, but wild animals often want some of what we have and to live in or near the places we call home. Yet like the baboon Peewee, we often hog the best stuff and the best places for ourselves and try to block others from getting anything but leftover scraps.

To improve life for wild animals, one of our biggest challenges is learning to accept and accommodate our wild neighbors where *we* live—in our own backyards.

This starts with adopting a mindset of tolerance and coexistence. It means not labeling certain animals as "pests"—like migrating geese, pigeons, snakes, squirrels, raccoons, rats, bugs, white-tailed deer, and tigers—just because we find them inconvenient. As we seek better ways to live together, we can respect nonhuman animals as sentient beings who are just trying to survive in a crowded world.

### *Protecting Animals from Us*

In fact, humans cause most wildlife conflicts. Our towns, cities, farms, roads, and railways gobble up former wildlife habitat, forcing animals to relocate while making crossing the landscape dangerous. For birds, cities and suburbs are almost "no-fly zones."

In the United States every year, around a billion birds die from colliding with buildings. The same windows that, for us, let in sunlight and provide views of nature can be an avian deathtrap. The solution is simple: Put stickers on windows and darken windows at night. Issues like these are ideal for citizen conservation. Many cities have groups like the NYC Bird Alliance, which coordinates volunteers who want to help.

There are other examples. In 2024 in Tamil Nadu, India, tenth-grader Sam Jefferson developed a device to help prevent wildlife deaths at railroad tracks. Deaths are common and include elephants. The device senses approaching animals and uses a siren and spraying water to drive them away.

On a larger level, conservationists are building "wildlife corridors" that include roadway overpasses and underpasses, so animals have safe passage; the biophilic cities movement seeks to make urban environments as green as possible. With a little effort and ingenuity, we can both protect animals and foster their inclusion in and around our communities.

How does a frog cross the road? Too slowly. In springtime, amphibians of all kinds migrate "home" to their birthplaces, and volunteer-run amphibian-crossing brigades help safely carry frogs and salamanders across the asphalt (see Get Started Resources).

Environmental journalist Brandon Keim joins in the "Maine Big Night." He says:

> To care about others is to be constantly reminded of how much pain and struggle there is in the world, and also how it is within each of our grasps to make a difference that is, for someone, world changing.

### *Fostering Coexistence*

Once upon a time, humans couldn't fence out wild animals. Everyday life meant coexisting with top predators like lions, tigers, and bears (*oh my!*).

This remains a daily routine in some indigenous communities today, and they can teach others how it's done.

It starts with the belief that animals are smart and have a right to be here. Knowing that wildlife can be dangerous, people adjust their behavior to protect themselves. But we humans must also accept that coexistence means accepting risk, whether that's losing goats to a predator or occasionally suffering attacks ourselves.

One example among many is an Adivasi tribe in southern India who live near wildlife sanctuaries in the Western Ghats. One elder explained:

> We are part of the animals. We have been living with tigers for centuries. We know tiger and elephant behaviors and they know ours. We know their smell and sound and we do not go to those places. Lots of birds ring alarm bells, so we move to different areas. Monkeys and langurs give call sounds. These are life skills. We look after the forest and leave some things for the animals. For example, we do not take all the honey. We leave some for the animals.

Exactly like learning how to cross the street to not get hit by cars, we can learn "life skills" that minimize wildlife conflicts. We wear seatbelts and set speed limits because tens of thousands of people die in vehicle accidents every year, but we don't banish cars. Nor do we need to banish wildlife.

For instance, in 2015, Pettorano sul Gizio, a tiny Italian village, decided to bear-proof the town. The surrounding mountains are home to critically endangered Marsican bears, who for over a century were killed and driven away due to damage and conflicts. But once the village added electric fences to protect farm animals, installed gates, used bear-proof garbage bins, and learned not leave food waste outside, bear-related damage dropped to almost zero. Now nature tourists flock to Pettorano, improving the economy, and eighteen other "bear-smart communities" have followed across Europe.

In San Francisco, coyotes have been residing within city limits for almost twenty years. While walking her dog, Janet Kessler ran into one in 2007. She was fascinated and started her own citizen-science project to study them. On a blog, she documents generations of pups arriving and surviving and has come to realize that, she says, "coyotes ultimately are not so different from us."

Calling herself the "coyote lady," Janet also shares with neighbors her tips for managing coyote encounters. What should you do? Be calm, control any pets, and give coyotes space without trying to scare them away.

In fact, resident coyotes are helpful neighbors. They feed on and drive away rats, raccoons, and other troublesome critters, and this provides safe haven for birds and other species, which increases biodiversity.

Remember this when you encounter wildlife around your home. Give animals respectful, safe space, knowing that tolerance benefits everyone.

# 8
# you've got a friend in me

## Love, Friendship, Trust, and Devotion

A lioness and her four cubs relax in the savanna, Serengeti National Park, Tanzania.
Photo courtesy of Thomas D. Mangelsen, Images of Nature.

Is there a more mysterious emotion than love?

Poets rhapsodize and musicians croon about it, but what is it? Don't ask a scientist. They'll start mumbling about neurochemistry and "reciprocal social bonds" as if they've never felt their heart beat fast.

Mostly, researchers avoid the subject entirely. Few name love as a primary or universal emotion; not even Darwin put it on his list.

But isn't love what makes the world go round?

One trouble with defining love is its many varieties. There are three main types: romantic love between mated partners, maternal love between parents and children, and filial love between siblings and friends. Among people, we can add love of animals and love of nature, in addition to every other object of our affection.

Whether nonhuman animals feel all these varieties is hard to know. Love has no facial expression. Gestures like hugs, caresses, and kisses can mean many things. Even when species mate for life, that might be hard-wired instinct, not intentional devotion.

Plus, if we struggle to define love, how can we recognize it in other animals?

Obviously, many animals feel love. The presence of grief proves it. Animals also exhibit a long list of behaviors that often accompany love: loyalty, affection, tenderness, pleasure, commitment, protectiveness, physical closeness, mutual caretaking, resource sharing, consoling gestures, trust, respect, and friendship, aka "reciprocal social bonds."

Simply put, love means seeking and enjoying someone's company. It means choosing to be with and care for someone. That is what these stories show.

—

## An Elephant's Kiss

Elephant greetings are genuine wildlife spectacles. When herds reunite, they engage in exuberant mosh pits of brassy trumpeting, spinning and bumping bodies, flapping ears, clacking tusks, and entwining trunks.

When individuals really want to show how much they care for each other, they place their trunk in the other's mouth—a gesture as common and intimate as a kiss.

In Etosha National Park in Namibia, biologist Caitlin O'Connell has witnessed many elephant reunions, and it doesn't seem to matter how long elephants have been apart. It might be days, hours, or even minutes. As she says, "Animal societies do not appear to exhibit 'greeting fatigue' like we often do."

One time O'Connell found her way blocked by Knob Nose, the matriarch of her family, and Donut, her second-in-command, when they reunited after being apart for *maybe* an hour. She says:

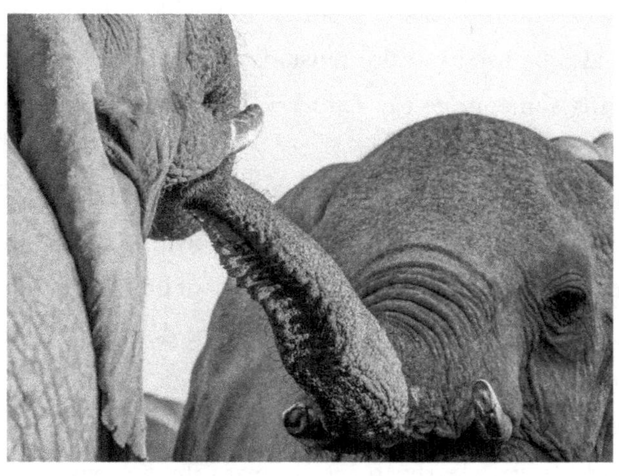
An adult female elephant greets a higher-ranking family member with a trunk-to-mouth greeting. Photo courtesy of Caitlin O'Connell.

> Facing each other, the elephants held their heads high above their shoulders while rapidly flapping their ears. Then Donut lifted her trunk and bellowed a thunderous roar, almost as if something terrible had just happened. Having observed wild elephants for as long as I had, I knew this vocalization was purely an expression of intense excitement.
>
> Next, the elephants rumbled softly while preparing to place their trunks in the other's mouth—the elephant equivalent of a handshake. Trunks extended, the tips of both of their trunks quivered in anticipation, as Donut gently placed the tip of her trunk against the side of Knob Nose's mouth like a kiss. Knob Nose reciprocated.

Imagine students doing *that* every time they met after class? But their greeting wasn't over. Knob Nose and Donut repositioned themselves side by side, shoulders high, trunks so relaxed the tips hit the ground, "while roaring and rumbling wildly." Then, O'Connell says, "the inevitable happened":

> No female elephant greeting ceremony is complete without the sudden and thorough evacuation of both bowels and bladder. It is the ultimate expression of sheer, elephantine joy.

### *A Kiss Isn't Just a Kiss*

The trunk-to-mouth ritual serves many functions. It can be a simple hello, like a high-five or an aunt's peck on the cheek. It can also be used to calm tensions and avoid a fight or to reconcile after one, not unlike hugging someone to say *I'm sorry*. Elephants adjust the gesture as needed to express a variety of positive feelings.

Among male elephants, O'Connell says it functions almost like kissing the ring "of the *capo di tutti capi*, a mob boss—even to the point of lining up and performing the act in single file, usually in order of dominance." O'Connell once watched elephant bulls gather to drink at a water trough, but none took a sip before they had kissed Greg, the dominant bull:

> Each bull approached in turn with trunk outstretched, quivering in trepidation, dipping the tip into Greg's mouth. It was clearly an act of great intent, a symbolic gesture of respect for the highest-ranking male.

We don't think of kisses as dangerous, but it's a very vulnerable gesture. That might be why kissing is such a powerful way to express affection. O'Connell says:

> Anyone witnessing this ritual for the first time quickly recognizes how trusting it is for an elephant to place the tip of its trunk in another's mouth. It's a risky behavior considering how sensitive the tip of an elephant's trunk is and how easy it would be to get bitten.

Elephants are very picky about their friendships, which can last lifetimes, and they create names for one another, something that, so far, has only been verified in parrots and dolphins. A 2024 study, which used AI to dissect elephant vocalizations, found that elephants have specific calls for individuals, and they recognize their own elephantine names.

Undoubtedly, elephants use names to track each other and coordinate movements. Elephants care about who they are with, and they will adjust their travel to remain with friends.

Ecologist Carl Safina says, "A major rule of elephant society is that individual personalities trump rules. Things happen because somebody likes somebody else and they want to hang out."

—

## Field Notes: Grooming David Greybeard

Jane Goodall climbs a tree to get a better view of chimpanzees, Gombe National Park, Tanzania. Photo by Hugo van Lawick.

In July 1960, when Jane Goodall first arrived in Tanzania's Gombe National Park, she didn't know how long the chimpanzee study would last. Year after year, it kept being extended, and today, over six decades later, it continues as the world's longest-running study of any nonhuman animal.

During the first years, Goodall worked tirelessly to build relationships with the chimps, and her most important relationship was with David Greybeard. His trust and acceptance of her encouraged other chimps to accept her as well. Without David Greybeard's leadership, cooperation, and eventual friendship, none of what followed might have been possible.

Goodall's reports from Gombe rocked the world. They not only transformed our understanding of chimpanzees—our closest kin—but of ourselves. She was the first to document that chimpanzees make and use tools. The first to discover that chimps eat meat and wage war. The first to show that chimpanzees display compassion and have strong mother/child bonds.

She was the first, in other words, to prove how similar humans and chimpanzees are on the inside—emotionally, behaviorally, psychologically, socially.

Here is the story of how Jane Goodall earned David Greybeard's trust.

### *Getting Closer*

During her first months in Gombe, Goodall could barely find any chimpanzees to study. She despaired over her inability, she said, "to overcome the chimpanzees' inherent fear of me, the fear that made them vanish into the undergrowth whenever I approached. At first they … fled even when I was as far away as five hundred yards and on the other side of a ravine."

Slowly, the chimps stopped fleeing, and she was able to make observations and identify individuals using binoculars. But getting too close triggered hostility and aggression.

During one rainstorm, she was a short distance from a chimp who hadn't seen her. Then she heard soft *hoos* and held still, realizing she was surrounded on all sides.

Goliath, the alpha male, was in a tree directly above her, and she says he "uttered a long drawn-out *wraaa*, and I was showered with rain and twigs as he threatened me, shaking the branches." All the other chimpanzees echoed the cry, which "is one of the most savage sounds of the African forest." A branch hit her in the head, a chimp charged and veered off at the last instant, then all the chimps vanished.

"I think I expected to be torn to pieces," she said.

Goodall persevered, testing boundaries and enduring aggressive displays that included screams, bluff charges, and even physical slaps. Sometimes she was forced to retreat.

Then one day, after about six months, she walked into what she thought was an unoccupied clearing to discover two males "sitting so close that I could almost hear them breathing." She recognized them as Goliath and David Greybeard, and they were "staring at me intently." She didn't move, the chimps didn't flee or attack, and after a moment, they returned to grooming each other.

The sun was setting, and David Greybeard stood and regarded Goodall as "my elongated evening shadow fell across him." She said:

> The moment is etched deep into my memory: the excitement of the first close contact with a wild chimpanzee and the freakish chance that cast my shadow over David even as he seemed to gaze into my eyes.

This moment inspired the title of Goodall's famous book *In the Shadow of Man*. Afterward, she experienced a turning point in her relationship with the chimpanzees. She said:

David Greybeard.
Photo by Hugo van Lawick.

> Once, as I was watching a group in a tree about thirty yards away, I heard a slight rustle in the leaves behind me. I looked around. There about fifteen feet away sat a chimpanzee with his back to me. I was motionless, thinking he had not seen me, but after a few moments he glanced casually at me over his shoulder, then went on chewing. He stayed there for another ten minutes, sometimes giving me a quick look, before finally walking away.
>
> Their original fear of me had gradually given place to aggression and hostility and now many of the chimps had begun to accept me as part of their normal, everyday landscape. A strange white ape, unusual to be sure, but not, after all, terribly alarming.

### *Going Bananas*

In spring 1962, after being away for six months to attend Cambridge University, Goodall returned to Gombe to find that "the chimps were, if anything, *more* tolerant of my presence than before," she said.

Then one day, David Greybeard visited their research camp. He climbed into an oil nut palm tree directly over Goodall's tent. Goodall said, after feeding on the fruit,

> ...he climbed down, paused to look, quite deliberately, into the tent, and wandered away. After all those months of despair, when the chimpanzees had fled at the mere sight of me five hundred yards away, here was one making himself at home in our very camp.

David returned periodically to dine in the palm trees. One time, he approached Goodall herself, to within five feet, "and slowly his hair began to stand on end, until he looked enormous and very fierce," she said. "A chimpanzee may erect his hair when he is angry, frustrated, or nervous. Why had David now put his hair out?"

All at once, David rushed forward, grabbed a banana from the table, and ran away to eat it. After that, the researchers left bananas out to encourage David to visit. For two months, he appeared at unpredictable times, even once bringing along Goliath. The alpha male was skittish but also kept returning.

One day when David came alone, Jane offered him a banana from her hand. He acted "mildly threatening"—putting his hair out, swaggering, and slapping a tree trunk—but Goodall remained calm, and David eventually, "very gently, took the banana from me."

After Goodall succeeded in getting the more-nervous Goliath to take a banana from her hand, some thaw broke. Small groups of chimps began coming to camp and hanging around. Yet this led to new troubles—the chimps stole clothes and cardboard and sometimes busted furniture and fought among themselves. In hindsight, Goodall wished she hadn't fed them bananas, since it changed their behavior, but at the time, she calmed the situation by devising a new system of delivering bananas using bins at the edge of camp.

For the first time, Goodall could observe individuals and groups at close range on a regular basis, and their research took off.

### *Touching Hands and Hearts*

Christmas Day 1962 was "a day to remember," Goodall said. She set out huge bunches of bananas, and several chimps came to feast. Then David Greybeard arrived by himself.

> I sat close beside him as he ate his bananas. He seemed extra calm, and after some time I very slowly moved my hand toward his shoulder and made a grooming movement. He brushed me away—but so casually that after a moment I ventured to try again. And this time he actually allowed me to groom him for at least a minute. Then he gently pushed my hand away once more. But he had let me touch him, tolerated physical contact with a human being—and he was a fully adult male chimpanzee who had lived all his life in the wild. It was a Christmas gift to treasure.

We don't know what David Greybeard was thinking and feeling. Among chimpanzees, grooming is a complex behavior. It's almost like currency, something to give and receive in exchange for food or favors. It is also a way to bond and communicate friendship, caring, and trust.

As Goodall had experienced, closeness itself wasn't accepted lightly, and touch is even more intimate. After this moment, another breakthrough occurred: David allowed Jane to follow him into the forest, rather than threatening her away as he had before.

Through his example over the years, David continued to encourage other chimps to accept Goodall and the researchers. This culminated in Flo allowing Goodall and her husband, Hugo, to wrestle with and tickle her infant son, Flint. Goodall "marveled" at this mother's level of trust, which was another high point of chimpanzee acceptance, and in the moment, she didn't see any harm in physical play.

However, Goodall later discouraged physical contact, calling it "foolish." If chimpanzees became too acclimated to humans, it would affect their behavior, and encouraging physical interactions could be dangerous, since adult chimpanzees are incredibly strong and could easily hurt a person by accident.

David Greybeard died in 1968 during a pneumonia epidemic. For Goodall, his passing meant losing not just the most-important chimpanzee to the success of the Gombe study, but a genuine friend. David is credited with many firsts—the first to accept Goodall's presence, the first to visit camp, to take a banana, to permit human touch, and more. Perhaps most of all, he seemed to enjoy, foster, and want Goodall's companionship.

Goodall said:

> I do not regret my early contact with David Graybeard; David, with his gentle disposition, who permitted a strange white ape to touch him. To me it represented a triumph of the sort of relationship man can establish with a wild creature, a creature who has never known captivity. In those early days I spent many days alone with David. Hour after hour I followed him through the forests, sitting and watching him while he fed or rested, struggling to keep up when he moved through a tangle of vines. Sometimes, I am sure, he waited for me—just as he would wait for Goliath or William—for when I emerged, panting and torn from a mass of thorny undergrowth, I often found him sitting, looking back in my direction; when I had appeared, he got up and plodded on again.

—

## One of the Herd

In March 2006, Joe Hutto and his wife Leslye moved to Slingshot Ranch in Wyoming. Though they didn't realize it, their homestead was in the middle of the winter range of the region's mule deer, an iconic herd species of the American West.

Then one day in September, they looked out their kitchen window to find a large mule deer doe staring back at them. She was "a big healthy-looking animal with a beautiful coat," Hutto says, with "large, flirtatious eyelashes" and "dark brown eyes."

That winter, this curious doe inspired Hutto, an ethologist, to conduct what turned into an immersive seven-year study, during which he himself became one of the herd.

### *Curiouser and Curiouser*

Every afternoon, the doe returned. Hutto dubbed her Rayme. Soon, Rayme's family group arrived, but unlike Rayme, who showed no fear, the others kept their distance. On occasion, Hutto tossed "horse cookies" to Rayme, who liked them, and it wasn't long before Hutto would call her name and she'd "mysteriously appear within seconds."

Rayme also developed what Hutto calls a "peculiar habit." Their house had large, curtainless windows on all sides, and at night, Rayme would stare into them. Hutto says:

> Although a little disconcerting, we eventually realized that Rayme would literally follow us as we moved through the house, going from window to window, fascinated with our activities. At 10:00 p.m. you would look into the otherwise black square of a window and suddenly make out the face of a deer, almost pressed against the glass—there was Rayme—wide-eyed and watching our every move.

Her comfort increased. Each day, as Joe and Leslye went about their chores, she'd lie down, yards away, and chew her cud. Within weeks, an extended clan of fifteen mule deer were making themselves at home in their yard. Hutto says:

> Rayme somehow managed to make it perfectly clear not only that she was consumed with interest regarding our activities but also that she clearly wanted attention from us. There was something about our mere proximity that Rayme

desired. For reasons that will always remain a mystery, Rayme found us—Rayme sought us out.

Rayme's boldness and curiosity "opened a door I never knew existed," Hutto says. Echoing David Greybeard and Jane Goodall, Rayme's acceptance "bridged the divide between her family and ours," Hutto says, and he calls what happened next "her lasting legacy."

### *Bonding through Touch*

A male mule deer in the snow, Wyoming. Photo courtesy of Thomas D. Mangelsen, Images of Nature.

Once spring arrived, the herd dispersed into their summer range, and in winter 2007, the mule deer returned.

Sadly, Rayme was not among them. For reasons unknown, she did not survive, and Hutto tasted what became a familiar emotion—grief—as he bonded with the mule deer.

To his surprise, the returning mule deer remembered the names they'd been given and acted like regulars, and "the new, wide-eyed fawns were so accepting" it was as if they'd been told what to expect. One day, Notcha returned with some new does, but upon seeing Hutto, the group startled and ran. Hutto called out "Notcha!" She immediately stopped, left the other deer, and he says, "ran—yes, ran—at a gallop directly to me."

Hutto was astonished and asked himself: "Who am I actually dealing with here, and what *are* the possibilities?"

The first winter, Joe and Leslye hadn't tried to touch the mule deer, but now they couldn't help it. Does worried their pockets for horse cookies, and a few, like Notcha, sought out rubs, neck scratches, and grooming. Cappy would paw Hutto's backside if she felt ignored, while Rag Tag, as she was groomed, would bend around to groom Hutto by licking and nibbling his coat.

Hutto says:

> Mutual grooming is an important aspect of mule deer social interaction and bonding within the herd. A mule deer will not engage in mutual grooming with just any other individual deer, but rather will do so only with family members or the closest affiliates. Rag Tag was clearly conceding that I was a member of her most immediate family.

Hutto felt the mule deer were making an intentional decision to trust him and Leslye—and only them. If a stranger approached the house, they were "gone in a flash."

This didn't seem like habituation. Hutto witnessed "over and over again" how the mule deer transformed all at once from skittish to accepting. He says:

> Suddenly, one day, a deer who was previously fearful may in a single moment walk forward in an ordinary manner and take a cookie from your hand. It sometimes feels as if the deer has shrugged off its apprehensions in one single, conscious declaration of faith.

### *Walking into Another World*

In 2008, during the third winter, Joe and Leslye realized that "knowing—even loving—a wild mule deer was a double-edged sword." Cappy did not return, and they witnessed the excruciating death by illness of Raggedy Anne.

Then one afternoon, another breakthrough: Hutto casually trailed Peep as she browsed slowly, only to find he'd wandered a quarter mile from the house. Standing in the middle of the herd, Hutto realized that "these deer had not come into my life, but rather I had been admitted into theirs."

Hutto kept joining the herd as they left the house and discovered several interesting things. If he walked with them, they accepted his presence, but if they left without him, and he followed later, they became uncomfortable and shied away. He learned to approach individuals indirectly and to avoid sustained eye contact. Meanwhile, some deer who were fearful of Hutto in his yard would ignore him in the foothills and even browse unconcerned at his feet.

"Logically," Hutto says, "they were more comfortable with me in their world than when they had been with me, in mine."

Significantly, the mule deer never lost their vigilance to humans in general. On several occasions, a human silhouette appeared on the horizon, and he says, "I have almost been trampled by the explosive flight that has occurred."

Hutto says:

> There is absolutely nothing that I could do to compromise the deer's inherent wildness. These creatures are intelligent, entirely cognizant, and totally disinclined to ever jeopardize or betray their better instincts for survival.

Hutto alone was befriended by the mule deer in this way. And this drove home to him the same lesson that Jane Goodall learned: If a person is sensitive, respectful, patient, and kind, they might be accepted and trusted by a community of wild animals.

Provided with a window into another species, Hutto pressed his nose to the glass just like Rayme. This "privileged access to the animals' vision of the world," Hutto says, allowed him "to see the ecology from their perspective—from their point of view."

Hutto's walks with the mule deer continued each winter for the next four years.

> Every day I'd pack a lunch, kiss my wife goodbye, and head out to wander with the deer. They'd graze their way across the foothills, and I'd walk along with them. They'd bed down for a nap, and I'd lie down, too.

One afternoon, a mile from the ranch, standing among twenty mule deer, with only mountains and wilderness visible for a hundred miles, Hutto marveled at his own transformation:

> As they buried their heads back among the sagebrush and snow, I realized that I was occupying no more interest than any other member of the group. I was now living among mule deer.

### Childhood Inspiration: Wendy Townsend

Wendy Townsend is a member of the Iguana Specialist Group with the International Union for Conservation of Nature. She lives with five West Indian rock iguanas in New York's Catskill Mountains, and she's authored three novels for young readers: *Lizard Love, The Sundown Rule,* and *Blue Iguana.*

> I saw my first lizard in Mooresville, Indiana, when I was six years old. One hot day I was sitting on the ledge that went around the pool. Something made me look over by the dogwood tree behind a low brick wall. I saw a dark, glossy-scaled creature slip out of a crack. Thin gold stripes went nose to tail. She moved in spurts, her arms and legs making tiny bursts of energy. I kept still and watched her flitting along the edge of the brick wall, breathless with wanting her to come closer. She moved like no animal I had seen, not just her ready-to-flee tense moves, but everything about her. She was miraculous. When a crow flew overhead, she streaked across the patio and disappeared at the edge. Hot Weather Lizard, I called her, because I saw her only on hot days.
>
> During those early years I was figuring out that animals had differences and similarities. The baby rabbits who ran out of their nest when my grandfather's tractor came close were like the mice who lived in the pumphouse by the pond. I held baby starlings who fell out of the nest holes in the martin houses; they were the same as birds at the feeders.

Moths, spiders, and dragonflies were bugs. The wet-and-dry animals were a special group. They were tadpoles, frogs, toads, salamanders, turtles, and snakes. My five-lined skink belonged in this group, the reptiles and amphibians. They were my people.

I would identify myself as a person who must live with iguanas for my emotional well-being. Iguanas keep me connected to wild places. They soothe my grief over lands that are disappearing and keep alive in me curiosity and hope. Writing is how I give iguanas a voice. Most of us have dogs for companion animals, but for me, the slow, quiet time and space required to get to know iguanas is where I've always needed to be. I prefer to enter their world to find out who they are. I don't ask them to figure me out or please me.

## Mother Bear: Queen of the Tetons

Bear 399, Grand Teton National Park, Wyoming.
Photo courtesy of Thomas D. Mangelsen, Images of Nature.

For centuries, grizzlies have had an infamous reputation as terrifying "maneaters." It's in their Latin name, *Ursus arctos horribilis*—the horrible bear.

That reputation is horribly unfair.

In the Grand Tetons, one grizzly became famous because of her tolerance and mothering. In fact, Bear 399 became such a bona fide celebrity she was dubbed the world's most-famous bear.

Her story is, first of all, about the love and devotion of motherhood. But it's also about sharing a landscape. Bear 399 was an extraordinary matriarch who showed everyone how people and wildlife might coexist.

### *Her Most Devoted Fan*

It's safe to say that 399 wouldn't have become an international star without the love and devotion of world-renowned wildlife photographer Tom Mangelsen.

In 2006, Tom heard that a mother grizzly with three newborns had been sighted in the Grand Tetons. A resident of Jackson Hole, Wyoming, Tom had never seen a grizzly that far south within the Greater Yellowstone region.

He took the first known photograph of 399, as she and her cubs fed on an elk carcass, and says, "Little did I know that that day was the beginning of a … relationship that would make 399 my favorite subject in my fifty-year career of photography."

As 399 and her cubs began frequenting the roadsides around Jackson Lake Lodge, locals and tourists noticed, and speculation grew that she was deliberately choosing to stick near people to protect her cubs as she raised them.

In 2004, Bear 399—who had been numbered by federal wildlife biologists when they tagged her for tracking—gave birth to a cub who died that same year. Unrelated male grizzlies are known to kill cubs (so they can mate with the mother), and some felt that might have been what happened. Living near people was probably 399's method for avoiding male grizzlies (who avoid us).

Tom Mangelsen at work, Grand Teton National Park, Wyoming. Photo by Tiffany Talbott, courtesy of Thomas D. Mangelsen, Images of Nature.

Yet her proximity was troubling. If she habituated to humans, and started eating human food, she might suffer the fate of most bears who are perceived as threats: She'd either be relocated or euthanized.

### *Kindness Begets Kindness*

In spring 2007, 399 emerged from hibernation with her now one-year-old cubs and grew even bolder. She often lounged, fed, and played with her cubs near roadsides, causing "bear jams" as dozens of cars stopped and people gaped in awe. One early evening in Willow Flats, in view of Jackson Lake Lodge, 399 emerged to teach her young how to hunt elk as a herd grazed in the meadow.

Tom's photos of that incredible scene launched 399's fame.

Then in June 2007, 399 seemed to realize everyone's worst fears: She attacked a person.

While hiking in Willow Flats, Dennis VanDenbos accidentally stumbled upon 399 and her cubs feeding on an elk calf. Startled, 399 charged but stopped next to him without touching him.

As she loomed above, VanDenbos says, "I could now see all those teeth and the side of her head in silhouette and the hair on her back.... It was, in its own way, very beautiful."

VanDenbos retreated quietly, but after several steps, he tripped. The fall triggered 399, who bit at his backside. At first, VanDenbos says, "I had the sense it was just a warning." These weren't tearing bites. Then VanDenbos saw the cubs behind her, as if awaiting instructions, and VanDenbos was sure he was going to be killed.

Just then, another hiker saw the attack and screamed, and 399 and her cubs ambled away.

Park rangers were ready to kill 399, and would have, except that VanDenbos radioed to stop them. In his own act of kindness, he took responsibility for provoking the attack and said he wanted the bears spared.

Afterward, a member of the grizzly study team said: "If [399] wanted to treat him as prey and make it a lesson in hunting for her cubs, she would have. I think she probably was teaching her offspring. She showed them how a bear can respond nonlethally to people when humans represent a threat to them and their food source."

399's restraint—her apparent decision to spare VanDenbos's life and so provide a lesson in coexistence to her cubs—cemented admiration for her around the world.

And she never again attacked or threatened people.

### *Lessons in Motherhood*

In 2008, 399 weaned her now-two-year-old cubs by driving them away. Sadly, only one cub, labeled 610, has survived to today, but 610 has proven to be her mother's equal.

In 2011, 399 gave birth to a second set of triplets, and 610 emerged from hibernation with two cubs. The collective brood sometimes shared carcasses together, and they even hunted elk not far from each other in Willow Flats, drawing mobs of onlookers.

Meanwhile, perhaps because 399 was overwhelmed by her triplets, 610 "adopted" one of her mother's cubs, so she raised three and her mother only two. This "coparenting" arrangement was rare to the point of being unique, since wild animals typically only ever adopt motherless orphans.

399 taught her cubs how to be savvy within human-occupied land. One lesson was to follow hunters during elk-hunting season, so they'd get an easy meal by feasting on the gut piles left by hunters. And she taught her kids how to safely use and navigate "bear jams."

Tom says:

> I've watched 399 pause by the side of the road, look both directions, vocalize to her cubs, and when the coast was clear, lead them across the highway, sometimes returning to scold them when they stopped to play with the traffic cones they considered chew toys. If her cubs wandered off, she'd become frantic, calling out like a mother who may have lost a toddler in the supermarket.

These lessons came from bitter experience.

In 2012, one of her cubs was hit and killed by a car, and in 2016, the same thing happened to that year's cub, named Snowy. Tom says 399 behaved "as any grieving mother would." He told Marc:

> 399 dragged Snowy, holding her limp body in her mouth, and lay her next to a fallen spruce. She then returned to the highway, ran up and down frantically, foaming at the mouth, and bawled loudly over her infant's fate. She continued her mourning until sunrise. When highway traffic started picking up, the authorities distracted her in order to retrieve Snowy's body in fear of 399 also getting struck by a vehicle.

Such raw expressions of grief show how deeply 399 loved her children. Each cub mattered, and she devoted her life to them.

In 2023, she gave birth to the last of her eighteen cubs—whom Tom named Spirit. 399 was then twenty-seven and the oldest and most prolific mama bear ever observed in the Greater Yellowstone region. The bear equivalent of a great-grandmother, she and Spirit were often seen playing and wrestling, since Spirit didn't have siblings.

At the time, Tom said, "It's as if, like humans, she realizes the act of playing is important in many ways to the health and well-being of her young."

He added, 399 is "a mother who is exhibiting good family values, giving her offspring the same skills and instincts she possesses.... It's bears like her that are important to the survival of the species."

A "bear jam" in Grand Teton National Park.
Photo courtesy of Thomas D. Mangelsen, Images of Nature.

### *Bear Jams: Negotiating Coexistence*

The bear jams started in 2007, and like many outdoor music festivals, they grew in size and zaniness every year. Helping to keep crowds under control was the Grand Teton Wildlife Brigade, but Tom himself was often on hand—telling stories and warning people to stay back and act respectfully.

399 was proving she could handle herself near humans, but people often didn't behave responsibly around her.

Professor Susan Clark once said:

> Around her are all these things going on—people moving in and out of her space, conveying different kinds of messages through body language. There are smells of human foods drifting in the breeze. There are vehicles moving at various speeds. There is nervous tension in the air. Given all of this, 399 is making assessments in her own mind, hundreds of them, that inform what she is going to do. I see an animal that exhibited remarkable composure in showing her cubs how to move through the chaos.

Like 399 and 610, many of their offspring have exhibited the same nonchalance around people. One big lesson, says journalist Todd Wilkinson, is that "bear behavior is triggered by human behavior; the smarter that people behave, the smarter and more predictable bears do."

Like any relationship, but especially one between two of Earth's apex predators, successful coexistence is a two-way street.

That's not a metaphor. In the Greater Yellowstone region, roadways are a significant hazard and source of wildlife/human conflicts.

Bears outside park boundaries are increasingly using highways and suburban corridors to travel. This survival strategy makes people nervous. Using a technique called "hazing," authorities will try to drive away unwanted bears using loud sounds and bangs. In some cases, they tranquilize and relocate bears or even euthanize them.

The trouble is, relocated bears are sometimes placed in areas already occupied by other bears, so they have to keep moving.

Wildlife overpasses and underpasses are one solution. These provide safe ways for wildlife to cross highways and reach viable wilderness. In Greater Yellowstone, some already exist, and more are being planned.

### *399's Legacy*

We have to keep doing our part. When wild animals live near us, they will always require our help and attention. Even for bears like 399 and 610, knowing how to cross a road and avoid human conflict isn't protection enough. In 2023, 610 was hit by a truck and severely injured, though she recovered and is doing well today.

Tragically, in 2024, Grizzly 399 was hit by a car and killed along a road about fifty miles south of Grand Teton National Park. According to reports, the driver, who survived, was sober and going the speed limit, making this an unfortunate accident—one that caused mourning worldwide.

Yet it was an accident that might have been avoided. Tom told Marc:

> Authorities knew from photos and videos taken by commuters and from phone calls that 399 and Spirit had dragged a road-killed elk carcass off the highway the day before and were feeding on it. They knew the bears had been seen in the area and along the highway for weeks. I firmly believe that 399's death was avoidable had local and federal authorities acted responsibly and removed the elk carcass and hazed 399 and Spirit away from the dangerous highway. Even after 399's body was hauled off, the authorities didn't put up any flashing signs or patrol the area to warn motorists about a bear cub possibly wandering on the highway looking for their mom.

Spirit (whose gender is unknown) hasn't been seen since 399 was killed. While the yearling cub was old enough to survive on their own, Tom says, "It is more likely Spirit was also struck and killed the same night, and the cub either limped off into the woods or this was never reported."

Journalist Todd Wilkinson says that "the journey of 399 and her offspring may be the most closely documented of any wild grizzly family in human history." She earned our attention by being a loving, devoted mother who taught her children how to coexist with us—something we should foster, not fear.

For Tom Mangelsen, 399 was family. Though admitting that he can't know, Tom says, "I think she recognized my smell. She would cross in front of my car more often than others. I think she felt safe when she smelled our vehicles."

Tom concludes:

> Maybe once in a lifetime an animal like this appears and her mere presence seems to galvanize everything. An icon of motherhood. An emblem of wildness. A sentient creature who has taught us new ways to think about others of her kind....
>
> We can only hope that human tolerance prevails and leads to a wider acceptance of wild things—especially predators like bears, wolves, and cougars—that are not always convenient to live with. As 399 and 610 show, they are important, sentient beings, with intellect, feelings, and emotions just like us. They are not only crucial in a truly healthy ecosystem but also belong among us in their own right. Their acceptance into our midst is what makes us human.

Bears stand to improve their senses, like sight and smell, not to intimidate. Here, Bear 399 guards her weeks-old cubs in Grand Teton National Park. Photo courtesy of Thomas D. Mangelsen, Images of Nature.

—

## Get Started: Compassionate Conservation—Who Lives, Who Dies, and Why

Conservation, almost by definition, is driven by compassion and love for wild animals. The goal is to protect and preserve nature and to keep endangered species from becoming extinct.

This is vital, urgent work. Because of habitat destruction, pollution, invasive species, and human impacts (like hunting), Earth is experiencing what has been called "the sixth extinction." This means the current wave of extinctions is so vast and sudden, it may rival what's happened only five other times in Earth's history.

You might notice that all the main causes are linked to us, including invasive species. These are typically nonnative species, like rats, who humans have spread around the globe. That makes people even more determined to fix the damage we've caused.

The hard question is how.

### *Traditional Conservation: Prioritizing Species Over Individuals*

Some of the most effective conservation efforts involve protecting existing species within their current habitat and allowing populations to recover on their own. Usually, what wildlife needs most is enough space, a healthy environment, and freedom from us.

That isn't always possible, and conservation efforts also directly manipulate ecosystems. One way is by relocating endangered species to a new place—usually an area where the species once lived in the past. When successful, this helps restore and "rewild" damaged ecosystems.

Another approach is to eliminate nonnative, invasive species, especially when those animals are directly responsible for driving native species to their grave.

However, relocating species and killing invasive species involve more animal deaths. When species are reintroduced, they sometimes don't survive, in part because habitats have changed too much and people don't want them (such as wolves and bears). These new/old species can also impact current residents, thus causing fresh problems.

Meanwhile, exterminating nonnative, invasive species can involve prolonged, extensive killing campaigns that often fail, since it's hard to uproot a successful species. These efforts can also inflict collateral damage on many other animals.

Beyond effectiveness, these strategies raise larger ethical questions: Is it okay to kill some animals, or many animals, to save a species? Is it acceptable to reintroduce species to a new place knowing that some might die in the hopes that some might succeed?

Many conservationists think so. Traditionally, saving species and protecting biodiversity are considered more important than the well-being of individual animals.

### ***Compassionate Conservation: Each Individual Matters***

Marc doesn't agree, and he supports a rapidly growing global discipline called compassionate conservation. This view of conservation proposes that efforts to protect biodiversity should be guided by four principles:

1. first do no harm,
2. individuals matter,
3. value all wildlife, and
4. peaceful coexistence.

The Hippocratic oath—first do no harm—is the pledge all doctors make. It means that it can be better to do nothing than take an action that might cause more harm than good. To save wildlife, people have a long history of well-meaning efforts to engineer nature that then backfire and make things worse.

"Individuals matter" and "value all wildlife" mean that each being has intrinsic or inherent value and shouldn't be sacrificed for the "good of the species." So-called invasive species and pests also have intrinsic value and their lives should be respected. We are the ones judging species as good or bad, friend or enemy, and our judgments are emotional, often self-centered, and change depending on the context. Wolves were once reviled, and sometimes still are, even as many people now love and cherish them. Hedgehogs are spiky bundles of cuteness that, on some Scottish islands, have become nonnative villains who are decimating native birds. Friend or enemy?

Finally, "peaceful coexistence" means that, when there are human/wildlife conflicts, the needs of both people and nonhuman animals must be respected and accounted for. Conservation efforts never work if they don't also benefit people. If those who live with wildlife don't experience any value in protecting animals or nature, they won't.

Finding a solution that fulfills all these goals isn't easy, but it can be done. One example is in Bolivia, where biologist Ximena Velez-Liendo is working with local communities to help preserve Andean bears. As villagers expanded into the bear's habitat, converting more land for farms, they treated the bears as pests who threatened their livestock and crops. Yet Velez-Liendo is convincing locals to preserve bear habitat and stop killing bears by training them to become beekeepers instead of farmers. By producing honey, locals earn a living that doesn't impact the welfare of Andean bears.

Ultimately, saving wildlife and restoring nature is very complex, and every conservation effort requires its own unique solution.

What can be hard to face is our own sense of guilt and responsibility. No matter how much we want to help, at times there are no good choices, only less-bad ones. Though we might want to preserve nature and animals exactly as they are, change and loss are inevitable, no matter what we do.

Yet we can always make sure that our decisions uphold our values. This is our constant challenge. So consider your values and keep them in mind every time you face a choice about what to do.

# 9

# help! i need somebody

## Altruism and Gratitude

In December 1925, the Siberian husky sled dog Balto met "Balto," the statue of himself erected in Central Park, New York City. Ten months before, driven by Gunnar Kaasen (left), Balto had led the final sled run to Nome, Alaska, in the midst of a blizzard, delivering antitoxin during a diptheria epidemic that saved the town. At the time, Kaasen told newspapers, "I couldn't see the trail. Many times I couldn't even see my dogs so blinding was the gale. I gave Balto, my lead dog, his head and trusted to him. He never once faltered.... It was Balto who led the way, the credit is his." Photo by Smith Archive/Alamy.

Altruism—sacrificing something significant to help someone else—is a powerful expression of compassion and love. This can be the running-into-a-burning-building-to-save-a-baby type of heroism or the more everyday giving-up-an-evening-to-help-a-friend-study form of generosity. The key is that we put someone else's needs above our own.

While any selfless gesture might be considered altruistic, the ultimate example is when we save someone's life even at the risk of our own life or welfare, particularly when we help strangers. This is what first-responders do every day and why we celebrate and honor them. This type of willing self-sacrifice for others is considered one of humanity's highest virtues.

This—rather than the ability to fly or spin webs—is what makes superheroes heroic.

The question raised by this chapter is whether other animals share this impulse. Might humanity's highest virtue not be ours alone?

Scientists are very reluctant to admit that nonhuman animals display altruism. For animals, they define altruism in very limited, utilitarian terms—as selfless behavior that benefits the recipient at the cost of the altruist's fitness. By "fitness," scientists usually mean the ability to reproduce, and "selfless" means there can't be *any* potential self-interest, like protecting one's own child (and thus one's genes).

While many species display compassion and helping behaviors, it's extremely rare for us to witness animals saving other animals who don't benefit them at all and in ways that genuinely risk their own survival.

But occasionally we do.

This chapter's stories also highlight gratitude. When helped by us, some animals seem to express thanks. This might indicate that they recognize selfless compassion when they receive it, and recognition implies they might be capable of altruism themselves—even if we aren't around to see it.

—

## Cat Versus Dog

When animals surprise us—when they do something we didn't think they would or even could—that usually says more about us than the animal. It's a sign that, perhaps, we haven't been paying close attention.

Take cats.

They have a reputation as … how to put it: Self-centered? Superior? Disinclined to help?

The sayings are endless:

"Dogs have masters, cats have slaves."

"Dogs come when they're called. Cats take a message and get back to you."

"The ancients worshipped cats like gods. They haven't forgotten."

Then a story comes along that demonstrates that cats love and care and will, when it matters, put themselves on the line for us.

Tara is one such cat. Her heroic rescue of a boy being mauled by a dog was captured on video, which forever put to rest the slander that cats only pretend to like us for their own benefit.

### *One Good Rescue Deserves Another*

The story starts in 2008 in Bakersfield, California. Roger and Erica Triantafilo were in a local park when a tiny bundle of fur galloped over, wanting to play. On their way home, the six-month-old kitten trailed after the couple. Several days later, when the homeless kitten still hadn't left, Roger and Erica realized they'd been adopted. They named the kitten Zatara—Spanish for "driftwood," and shortened to Tara—and let her in for good.

In 2009, Roger and Erica had their first child, Jeremy. Tara warmed to him immediately; she checked on him when he cried and slept with him in his crib. In 2012, the couple gave birth to twin boys, and Tara remained a remarkably loving and "mellow" cat, as Erica calls her. Despite being pushed, pulled, and even sat on, Tara never hissed at or scratched the boys.

Tara was and is particularly close to Jeremy, who is mildly autistic. Like Betsy and Rowan, it's possible that Tara recognizes that Jeremy's mind isn't exactly like others.

Flash forward to May 13, 2014. Jeremy had come home from school and was riding a balance bike up and down the driveway. Erica was watering plants, and Tara was lounging in the garden. The neighbors opened their gate to drive their car, and their one-year-old dog, a Labrador/Chow mix, raced out, spotted Jeremy, and attacked.

The dog bit and held Jeremy's leg, shook him, and dragged him off his bike. Within two seconds, before Erica could react, Tara flew down the driveway and plowed paws up into the dog's side, causing him to let go. When the dog didn't retreat fast enough, Tara charged again and chased him off for good. Then Tara abruptly U-turned and ran back to where Jeremy was being helped by his mother.

Jeremy needed stitches but recovered fully, yet Erica wasn't sure what she'd seen. The confrontation, she said, was "just a blur." So, Roger checked their home security cameras, and sure enough, there was the encounter, caught on film.

### *A Celebration Fit for a Dog*

Roger posted an edited version of the footage on YouTube, entitled "My Cat Saved My Son," and it registered 20 million views globally in five days.

Bakersfield declared June 3 "Tara the Hero Cat Day," Tara was named the grand marshal of the 2014 Bakersfield Christmas parade, and Tara and her family appeared on the *Today Show*. There is no such thing as an official "hero cat" award, so the Los Angeles ASPCA awarded her their National Hero Dog Award—scratching off "dog" and etching in "cat" on the plaque.

Not bad for five seconds of selflessness.

Despite people's surprise, recent research shows that cats can be trained like dogs, they can provide therapeutic interventions like dogs, and when people make the effort to bond with their cats, their cats bond with them, just like dogs.

Maybe Tara wouldn't save every four-year-old boy, but she didn't think twice about saving her boy, even from an out-of-control canine. Family is family and cats care, even if they're too cool to show it every second of every day.

—

## Dolphin Versus Shark

August 28, 2007, was a dreary, gray Tuesday morning at Marina State Beach, near Monterey, California. The waves were middling, but the ho-hum conditions didn't stop five surfers, including twenty-four-year-old Todd Endris, from surfing. Nor did they deter a pod of dolphins from riding the waves alongside them.

The dolphins "were swimming around us and swimming in front of and underneath us in a couple feet of water," Todd said. "There's always dolphins, but I didn't think anything of it. I thought they were being playful, you know, like normal."

Things were not normal.

### *Predator in the Shallows*

Around 11 am, Todd caught a wave and paddled back to the lineup. Watching the other surfers, he didn't see till the last second the sixteen-foot great white shark racing toward him.

A surfer and coastal bottlenose dolphins near Los Angeles.
Photo copyright © 2025 maddalenabearzi/OCS (under NOAA permit).

"It was so powerful and graceful," Todd said, "so fast and effective. He lifted me out of the water and bit down twice on me—once while I was in the air and once while I was going back into the water.... There was no pain on impact. There was a bottom jaw underneath my board and the top jaw pretty much like clamped on my thigh."

Wes Williams, a friend of Todd's, looked back when he heard Todd scream. Todd was being thrashed around inside a bunch of circling dolphins, and Wes thought, "What did he do to piss off the dolphins?"

"Then," Wes continued, "I noticed blood seeping out into a circle in the water, and I knew there was a shark down there. I started paddling in as fast as I could toward shore."

Todd hit the shark with his fist as he was whipped back and forth and briefly pulled underwater, but, he said, it "was like punching a Chevy Suburban covered with sandpaper. I was getting nowhere."

"Meanwhile," Wes said, "the dolphins were doing these big tail slaps on the surface of the water, and it was so bloody.... All of a sudden, one dolphin leapt full out of the air and swung its tail around, missing Todd's head by two inches. That would have killed him if it hit. It looked like a cartoon."

Unexpectedly, the shark released and didn't bite again. At that point, Todd's impression was that the dolphins were swarming to form "a wall between me and the shark where he couldn't get back to me."

Todd yelled, "Help me!"

### *Uncommon Courage*

Not a minute had passed.

Hearing his friend call out, Joe Jensen reversed course and paddled into the bloody attack zone to get Todd, shouting, "Grab your board! Grab your board!"

Joe helped Todd catch the next swell into the beach, where Wes and another friend, Brian Simpson, were waiting.

Wes and Brian applied pressure to Todd's wounds, which were gruesome. Todd's back was a serrated flap that exposed his spine and internal organs, and his right leg was punctured to the bone. Brian wrapped a tourniquet around Todd's upper thigh to stop the hemorrhaging. Still, Todd was incredibly lucky. Somehow, the shark's teeth missed rupturing his pleural cavity and his femoral artery, either of which would have killed him.

Then Todd's friends kept him conscious and calm until, minutes later, paramedics arrived, soon followed by a medivac helicopter, which flew Todd to the nearest hospital. In the end, Todd lost half his blood by the time he reached the surgery room, and putting him back together required six hours, five hundred stitches, and two hundred staples.

During his recover, Todd jokingly called himself "Shark Boy." He considered it a miracle he survived. "Too many things came together right for it to be called coincidence."

Most of all, Todd expressed gratitude for his friends—"I was the luckiest guy to have those three out there"—and for the "truly remarkable dolphins" who drove the shark away.

### *The Mystery of Live-Saving Dolphins*

After the shark attacked, Todd said, "The dolphins went absolutely nuts ... like they were my best friend. They tried to protect me at the cost of their family members and their babies. There were all kinds of small dolphins around."

The question is: Did the dolphins really intend to save Todd? Why would they, even if they recognized him as a fellow wave rider? Or were they actually protecting themselves?

Could both things be true?

Dolphins have a long history of saving humans from shark attacks and from drowning. Stories go all the way back to ancient Greece. In most incidents involving sharks, dolphins circle people to prevent attacks before they happen. But on rare occasions, as with Todd, dolphins have driven sharks away even after an attack began.

Which makes it seem like self-interest isn't the only reason dolphins thwart shark attacks, since they could easily swim away once a shark picks a person for their next meal.

Of course, dolphins might sometimes swim away, and we don't notice. All we really know is what we experience, which is that, occasionally, dolphins risk their welfare to save another species, us.

Remarkably, Todd didn't resent the shark. And afterward, he spoke out about the need to protect both sharks and dolphins. Sharks have "been on Earth millions of years," he said. "A whole lot longer than we have.... We're in his realm, not the other way around."

—

## It's a Bird, It's a Plane, It's ... Humpback Whales!

This story raises the question: Are humpback whales the good Samaritans of the seven seas? Dolphins save humans, but humpbacks save their fellow ocean-dwelling citizens.

In 2009, marine ecologist Robert Pitman was researching killer whales in Antarctica. One afternoon, his team witnessed some killer whales engaged in a confrontation with two humpback whales. After the killer whales left, they noticed a Weddell seal had been hiding between the humpbacks.

Strange, they thought.

They followed the killer whales, who soon tried to wash another seal off an ice floe. Yet the same two humpbacks charged in, wielding their flippers and driving the killer whales away.

This looked like "mobbing behavior," such as when birds collectively chase away a predator. Except that mobbing behavior is extremely rare among whales and had never been seen in humpbacks.

A few days later, it happened again.

Killer whales were trying to knock a Weddell seal off an ice floe, and a pair of humpbacks were nearby, agitated and bellowing. As the seal hit the water, one of the humpbacks rose from beneath, rolled on their back, and lifted the seal out of the water.

Were the whales actually trying to save the seal?

"We saw that at one point the seal had started to slip," Pitman recalls, and the humpback used a flipper "to gently nudge the seal back up onto its chest. Once we saw that, we knew it was no accident.... It looked like altruism—as if the whales were acting out of concern for the smaller animal."

A mother humpback whale and her calf.
Photo by Philip Thurston/iStock.com.

### *Did Anybody Else See That?*

Pitman was skeptical. The presumption of natural selection is that "animals always act in their own self-interest," he says. Saving seals doesn't help humpbacks. But if not altruism, what was their motivation?

Pitman launched a study and asked around: Had anyone else, citizen or scientist, witnessed this behavior?

Ultimately, Pitman collected 115 accounts told by fifty-four credible observers from 1951 to 2012 and realized that "there are records of this behavior wherever there are humpbacks."

One thing Pitman learned is that humpbacks have a reason to fear killer whales—or at least "transient" killer whales, who eat mammals. The subspecies called "resident" killer whales eat only fish, and they almost never have conflicts with humpbacks.

Transient orcas will hunt and kill infant and juvenile humpbacks, while adults are too big to attack. Adult humpback flippers are sixteen feet long, weigh a ton, and have knobby, barnacled edges that can destroy flesh. Along with their flukes, adult humpbacks are heavily armed.

Pitman theorized that humpbacks probably developed antipredator mobbing behavior to save their young. Once they hear killer whales attacking prey, even from as far away as two miles, humpbacks race to the rescue, not knowing who the orcas are attacking before they arrive.

Still, Pitman calls it "puzzling" and "perplexing" that humpback whales—once they realize that humpback calves aren't being threatened—don't just shrug and return to their regular lives. Witnesses logged around ten other species they'd seen humpbacks defend, including gray whales, minke whales, Dall's porpoises, sea lions, four species of seals, and ocean sunfish. Confrontations lasted from less than an hour to almost seven hours.

Observers marveled at the humpbacks' ferocity and determination. They were "swatting killer whales with their flukes," and "the trumpeting noise and quick forceful movements, directly at the orcas, was impressive."

Here is another account:

> We had traveled quite a distance to observe a group of killer whales attacking a gray whale mother and calf pair and out of *nowhere* a humpback whale came trumpeting in followed by another and then another until we had about five or more humpbacks.... It was strange because during the entire journey ... not a single humpback whale had been observed.... The result however was that the gray whale cow/calf pair was able to escape. [On other occasions] I also personally observed several sea lions surviving predation attempts as a result of humpback whales distracting killer whales.

### *Altruism by Any Other Name ...*

Pitman decided to call this behavior "inadvertent altruism," though it's also been called accidental or unintended altruism. Perhaps humpbacks learned to respond to killer whale attacks out of self-interest, to protect their children, but they still interfere even if it only helps other species. Maybe it's practice. While helping others interrupts a humpback's day and can result in minor wounds, no adult humpback has been seen suffering life-threatening injuries.

Without being able to read a whale's mind, maybe that's all we can claim. But the truth is, we can distinguish human altruism in similar ways: as self-interested when helping family and loved ones, and more "inadvertent" when we know helping strangers probably won't seriously risk ourselves.

Pitman's study concludes, the sources of cross-species altruism "could be a focus of future research."

Absolutely. Many exciting discoveries about animals lie ahead, and we hope some of this book's readers join these important efforts.

### Childhood Inspiration: Marlon Reis

Marlon Reis is an animal-rights advocate, and as the spouse of Colorado Governor Jared Polis, he is the First Gentleman of Colorado. Since 2019, he has worked with Marc on numerous statewide and national conservation projects, and he visits schools to discuss animal issues and advocacy with young people.

> As first gentleman of Colorado, I am often asked why I chose animal rights to be my cause. It's a fair question. Many first spouses across America choose more human-focused issues, like childhood hunger or mental health. Even after seven years in this role, I still don't have an easy answer. I've come to realize that my passion for helping animals isn't the result of a single defining moment or experience, but many.

I was one of those lucky kids who never had to ask my parents for a pet. I grew up in a house where the windows and doors were always open to the ceaseless comings and goings of animals. Birds sailed in and out, setting off chaos as our cats leapt floor to ceiling in gravity-defying pursuit. Then there were the neighborhood dogs, tempted into our kitchen by the promise of snacks doled out generously by my kid sister. Our family's open-door policy—welcoming the outside in, as it were—had the magical effect of making me feel at home in nature. Back then, playing meant going outdoors, and I'd spend hours marveling at the industriousness of ants; bumble bees alighting on dandelions; bats swooping at insects in the early twilight hours; and the silhouettes of racoon elders leading their kits single-file up the trees.

My parents always encouraged me to be more than just a passive observer of animals. I was one of them. It's that admiration for the natural world that made me the person I am today.

## A Knotty Question

Large sea creatures regularly get tangled in fishing lines and nets, which are harmful and potentially deadly. Lines cut into flesh, fins, and mouths, and weighted nets can be so heavy that air-breathing cetaceans can struggle to reach the surface.

Entangled animals also regularly approach humans as if asking for help. Then, when people do, animals patiently endure the painful process of being cut free, and afterward, they seem to acknowledge that help with behaviors that, to the people involved, feel like gratitude.

### *A Humpback Winks*

In December 2005, a female humpback whale got entangled in weighted crab lines that were so heavy she could barely keep her blow hole above water. A team of divers arrived to attempt a very dangerous rescue, since they had to swim next to and under the fifty-ton whale. If the whale reacted in fear or pain, any accidental whack with a flipper could kill them.

James Moskito, the first diver in the water, said, "My heart sank when I saw all the lines wrapped around it. I really didn't think we were going to be able to save it."

Moskito continued:

> Slowly swimming to the whale, getting closer and closer, inching my way, I put my hand right next to the whale, right next to the eye, … and I could see the eye was following me. *I'm here to help you. I'm not going to hurt you.*

The divers worked for over an hour. Again and again, they grabbed ropes, cut, and let the pieces sink. Moskito said:

> Some of the individual ropes went into the blubber two or three inches deep. I put my hand on the whale and I told the whale, *Okay, this is gonna hurt*. But the whale was so cooperative that it would open its mouth. [One] guy would put his hand up inside of it and pull pieces of rope out of the baleen one by one.

As Moskito worked around the whale's mouth, "its eye was there winking at me, watching me," he said. "It was an epic moment of my life."

Once the humpback was free, she didn't leave immediately. She swam in circles around and next to the divers, rubbing against them. "It felt to me like it was thanking us," Moskito said. Then the whale dove.

> The next thing I know I have this whale coming right up at me. And it was like a slow-moving bus.… It literally stopped six inches away from my chest, and then nudged me forward like your household dog does when he wants to be petted. It turned on its side and put its eye right next to me and stopped and looked. And I started petting her again. So it was definitely a feeling of affection.

### *A Manta Ray Remembers*

A diver and a manta ray swim together.
Photo by Elianne Dipp/Pexels.

For over two decades, conservationist Guy Stevens, who founded the Manta Trust, has been swimming with manta rays (who are fish, not mammals). He'd always heard stories of entangled mantas approaching divers as if asking for help, and in 2008, he had his own experience in the Maldives.

He was diving among a hundred mantas in a mass feeding, when one manta "swam directly to me, circling within inches of my head." He continued:

> The manta was a ten-foot-long female, and as she moved closer I saw that her injuries were severe. The line was wrapped around her body several times, slicing a wound about twelve inches directly through her upper and lower jaw, deep into her gill, and backward into her head. The more she tried to open her mouth to breathe and feed, the more the line dug into her flesh.

Stevens had to return to his boat for a knife and a new air tank. When he returned fifteen minutes later, the manta swam back to him. Stevens had to pull hard to remove the deeply embedded line in her head and gills, but "the manta remained calm throughout."

Once the line was removed, the manta kept circling Stevens, but he was out of air and only had time to snap some photos before surfacing. He dubbed her "Slice."

Over the next weeks, Stevens saw Slice several times. One time, during another mass feeding, Slice left the group and approached Stevens, circling him closely. Twelve divers were in the water, but she only approached him. Stevens didn't know what to make of her attention, but said, "I think Slice recognized me and was curious to learn and interact more with this strange creature who had helped to set her free."

Dolphins caught in lines are also known to approach divers. Which begs the question: Do sea creatures know people can and will untangle lines? Why else would they approach us so deliberately and then cooperate so readily?

Then again, in every story, people eagerly try to convey their good intentions, and maybe animals understand this nonverbal communication. They sense our compassionate desire to help and decide to trust us.

If that's so, maybe it's no surprise when we sense their gratitude.

## Young People Take Action

Entire books could be filled with inspiring stories of young people taking action on behalf of animals and nature. Here are three more. Also check out Jane Goodall's Roots & Shoots, Action for Nature's International Eco-Hero Youth Awards, and the Future for Nature Awards.

### Rylee Brooke: Promise to Our Keiki

Hawaiian environmental activist Rylee Brooke has been fighting for nature, wildlife, and the rights of children (keiki) since 2016, when she was eight. Early on, she says, "I found a lot of nonprofit organizations didn't want you volunteering with them." Adults assumed they would have to babysit kids, and regulations kept them from direct involvement. During book drives, "I wasn't actually allowed into the hospital to give kids the books until I turned sixteen."

Rylee says, "I had to make my own path."

She has spoken before government agencies on behalf of bills for environmental protection, shark and ray conservation, and cetacean captivity. She started the kid-run "Plastics Project" to help with beach cleanups, once collecting five hundred pounds of plastic in a day.

In 2022, she was a plaintiff, along with twelve other teens, in the world's first youth-led climate conservation lawsuit focused on pollution from transportation. In 2024, the group won a settlement with the Hawai'i government that established a constitutional right to a clean, healthy environment and that will hold the state's department of transportation accountable for achieving net-zero carbon emissions by 2045.

Rylee said at the time, "Today is a victory for us, the state, and every young person who believes in the power of their voice."

That's the goal of Rylee's "Promise to Our Keiki" program, which helps young leaders learn how to become effective advocates. When taking action, Rylee's advice is to keep it simple and set a date. The key is "really figuring out what you're passionate about."

### Richard Turere: Lion Lights

Richard Turere is a Maasai who grew up in Kenya, and from age nine, he started looking after the family's cattle.

"I'd take them out in the morning and bring them back in the evening," Richard says. "We put them in a small cow shed at night."

The region's lions are familiar with this routine. Cows in a pen are easy targets, and lions typically wait until night to attack. On Richard's farm, lions sometimes killed as many as nine cows a week. In fact, this is one of the main challenges to conserving African lions: They are shot by farmers in retaliation for livestock predation.

At age thirteen, Richard noticed something interesting: At night, the lions seemed afraid of his moving flashlight and wouldn't approach. So, he started tinkering with some broken flashlights and a motorcycle indicator box and created an automated light system that mimicked a human walking with a flashlight.

He called his invention "Lion Lights." It was so effective that others in his community asked for one, and as word spread, so did demand across Kenya.

Richard kept tinkering. He refined Lion Lights to use LED lights, solar-powered batteries, and varied light sequences to keep lions from detecting patterns. Ten years later, in 2023, Richard won a "Young Inventors Prize" from the European Patent Office. Lion Lights are now being used on thousands of farms in Kenya, Tanzania, Botswana, Namibia, Argentina, and India, and they deter not just lions but leopards, hyenas, and elephants.

Richard is extremely proud that his invention is helping meet the global challenge of wildlife conservation.

"I want this story to inspire the young kids that they too can do something," Richard says. "If I did it coming from this community with no education, and no resources whatsoever, then anyone can make it. Anyone can change this world."

### Romaan Jawwad: Safer Nets for Healthier Oceans

The Indus River in Pakistan is so muddy that, over millennia, the freshwater dolphins who call it home have evolved to be functionally blind. They make up for their sightlessness with echolocation.

One thing echolocation doesn't detect well is human fishing nets.

Of all the human impacts harming Indus dolphins, "the biggest threat to them is by-catch," says fifteen-year-old Romaan Jawwad from Lahore, Pakistan. By-catch refers to when dolphins get trapped in nets meant for fish, and they often die either in the nets or later due to injuries caused by the nets.

Using recycled materials, Romaan decided to help by developing an affordable prototype of a fishing net with "banana pingers." The ping from these automatic signaling devices can be heard by dolphins, alerting them to the nets.

"These nets are popular in developed countries," Romaan says. "However, they are not a common fishing practice in Pakistan. Being able to supply these nets to just eighty boats has led to the death toll to fall from twenty-five to twenty in a year."

Romaan calls her project "Safer Nets for Healthier Oceans." She is currently improving her prototype and trying to expand its adoption by local communities, while also advocating with local governments to improve enforcement of existing legislation to protect dolphins.

She says, "I believe youth has an important part in environmental activism because of their unique position in society, which allows them to combine new insights with innovative solutions.... Their commitment to environmental justice encourages community engagement and inspires collective action."

## Part of the Family

The message of this book is perfectly captured by the story of Willie Smits. In numerous ways, it embodies the power of compassion and altruism.

As a child, Willie felt an intuitive connection with animals. At two, he went missing and was found "hugging the meanest dog in the neighborhood," he says. Eventually diagnosed as mildly autistic, Willie developed a love of birds that lasted through high school. "I rescued many birds that had fallen from their nests, nurtured them, and released them back out into the world, some successfully."

He says, "I loved animals and could communicate love better with animals than with people."

In college, he got a degree in tropical forestry, and in 1985, he moved to Borneo to work for the Indonesian Ministry of Forestry. He got married, had two sons, and in October 1989, the couple was expecting a third child when Willie experienced a "connection that changed my life."

### *Saving Orangutans*

While shopping in an outdoor vegetable market, Willie was approached by a man trying to sell a baby orangutan in a cage. Willie refused and went home, but he couldn't shake the desperate look in the orangutan's eyes. "They penetrated me and got stuck in my soul," he says. "They were the force that led me back, the call for help."

That night, Willie returned after the market closed and found the baby, out of her cage, discarded on a garbage dump. She was gasping and near death. Willie took her home and stayed with her all night, massaging her and helping her drink watered milk. By morning, she started to recover.

Willie named her Uce. Two weeks later, someone asked him if he'd adopt another sick baby orangutan, Dodoy. Of course, he agreed.

Over the years, as Willie raised Uce and Dodoy, he says, "I noticed there wasn't a lot of difference between them and my own children; they reacted in the same ways." The orangutans understood human language, displayed abstract thought and love, and wordlessly communicated their own complex feelings. "They are so much like us."

A mother orangutan with her months-old child in Semenggoh Nature Reserve, Kuching, Borneo. Photo by nikpal/iStock.com.

Willie also learned about the plight of orangutans in Southeast Asia. They were used in medical research, forced to perform in boxing matches, kept as pets, and even eaten. Further, the wildlife conservation organizations at the time weren't very effective; they focused more on tourism than rehabilitation and protection.

"I decided to do something myself," he says, "to protect my Uce and Dodoy."

In 1991, he founded the Borneo Orangutan Survival Foundation (BOSF). For the first three years, support and funding were hard to find—with the remarkable exception of local schoolchildren. They tipped Willie off to orangutans who needed saving, and he says, "they donated their pocket money and did baking and spelling contests to raise money. They each gave tiny amounts—ten cents per month—but it kept me going."

Yet Willie knew, to save wild orangutans, he needed to think bigger.

### *Saving Rainforests and Saving People*

Wild orangutans live only on the islands of Borneo and Sumatra, where the rainforests were (and still are) being destroyed by illegal logging and burned down for palm oil production. Along with other endangered wildlife, Willie says, "Orangutans were in the way."

To save wildlife, Willie had to help save the rainforests, and to save the rainforests, people needed to benefit. Willie had to figure out a way for the rainforests to improve local Indonesian communities overwhelmed by poverty, crime, and unemployment.

"If you're hungry, you don't think about conservation," Willie says. "If you're hungry, you don't think about the future of a forest or orangutans."

It took decades of research, experimentation, and determination, but Willie discovered "the solution to my problem was the sugar palm." Sugar palms are a versatile food source—you can eat the palm heart and extract sugar from the sap—and cultivating them can provide income. Willie says:

> The goal of my sugar palm project was to take land that had been decimated, reforest it with indigenous trees, and plant sugar palms in and around it to produce a marketable product while creating a safe, sustainable primate habitat.

Willie first realized that vision at Samboja Lestari, an area razed for timber that "was grass desert with no wildlife at all," he says. As a diverse forest was restored, it became home to a thousand species, including rehabilitated orangutans, and the sugar palms provided jobs for thousands of people, whose incomes rose ten times what they were.

This model is being repeated.

### *Not Goodbye, See You Later*

Three years after Willie rescued Uce, she and Dodoy had learned the skills they needed to survive in the wild and were ready to be released, along with seven other rehabilitated orangutans.

They were brought to a protected forest. When the cages were opened, all moved quickly into the trees except one, Uce. She sat forlornly on top of her cage until Willie couldn't take it anymore.

> I went to her and led her to a *Licuala* palm. With my Swiss army knife I cut a leaf from its soft heart, ate some, and gave it to her. I stroked her for a while, and gradually she went up into the trees. She didn't want to go.

Uce wasn't seen again for over three years. The day she was spotted by BOSF staff, Willie rushed to see her.

> When she saw me, she came out of the trees, took me by the hand, and led me into the forest to a *Licuala* palm. With her teeth, she ripped out a leaf from the heart of the palm and gave it to me. I almost had a heart attack because that was exactly what I did for her.... I truly believe that she was telling me, "I remember."

Over the years, their reunions have continued and become even more poignant. The first two times Uce gave birth to a child, she approached Willie and put her babies in his arms, even though the infants were "terrified of me." As for Dodoy, he became the community's dominant male and fathered Uce's second son.

Like Samboja Lestari, the success of Uce and Dodoy is a model for how wildlife can be rescued and restored to their proper home in our modern world.

Willie knows better than anyone how much work and personal sacrifice this takes, and he's learned that "everyone has to participate." Yet he has a secret weapon:

I receive love and gratitude from my orangutan friends all the time. When I can, I walk into the forest, switch off my own language, and wait. My friends sometimes come down from the trees and greet me with happiness and hugs. They are gifts to our world. In protecting them, we are ensuring the survival of other species, too—including our own.

—

## Get Started: Rewilding in the Anthropocene

Our current geological era has been named the Anthropocene, which means "the age of humanity." That might sound like bragging, but it's not. Geological epochs are named after the main force shaping Earth's environment, and right now that's us.

Our presence is being carved into layers of sediment. Pollution, habitat destruction, species extinctions, megacities, climate change: Eight billion humans (and counting) leave a mark. The evidence can be read in the geological record.

This is nothing to be proud of. Marc calls the Anthropocene "the rage of inhumanity." Whatever the world's future, it has already been defined and will continue to be defined by us.

Yet as long as we're here, our story is unfinished.

We have work to do.

### *A Crisis of Coexistence*

It's not just individual animals—entangled whales, grieving cows, caged orangutans—who are asking for our help. It's entire species and ecosystems, which is overwhelming to consider. There are too many crises and seemingly more every day. But in essence, all these troubles boil down to one thing: a crisis of coexistence.

To take the widest perspective, humanity has not done a good job of taking care of the world we share with all beings. We have not been good neighbors, and our challenge is to become the opposite. Today, our goal should be to foster a healthy coexistence in which all beings have the space, ability, and circumstances to thrive.

That humanity has failed in this—so far—is partly unintentional. Over the last few millennia, we've solved so many problems related to survival that we have become, by any measure, the most successful species. Maybe the dinosaurs were as dominant back in their day, but probably not.

However, we've also been selfish and prioritized our own survival over other species. We've tried to eradicate species, like other top predators, and we've manipulated evolution to create domestic species who serve us. In terms of biomass, humans and domestic animals are now over ten times more prevalent than wild animals.

This is just one detail that illustrates how our world is out of balance. So how do we fix the scales?

### *Rewilding Our Hearts*

The most important thing is for each of us to act within the context of our own lives. This starts by adopting a mindset of compassion, which Marc calls "rewilding our hearts."

When Marc was growing up, he felt "unwilded" by school—by being "caged" in classrooms—and by an education and profession that said it was okay to kill animals to learn about them. He rewilded himself by refusing to harm animals—as much as possible, and whenever alternatives existed.

For an ethologist, the best education comes not from books but fieldwork—by observing species in nature living as they were born to do. Not coincidentally, "live and let live" is an excellent definition of what it means to be a good neighbor.

In practice, rewilding means walking through the world treating other beings as equals—not the same as us, but as having an equal right to life. It means fostering a heartfelt connection with other animals and with the magnificence of nature. It means dissolving the false boundaries between "them" and "us." It means living by the golden rule: Do unto others as you would have them do unto you. Who could possibly argue with that?

Rewilding also means being less selfish by not always thinking of ourselves first. It means, at times, practicing self-sacrifice so others can succeed.

Rewilding, in other words, is a form of altruism and an expression of gratitude.

Through rewilding, we celebrate and treasure the diversity of nature, knowing that coexistence benefits everyone, and we look for ways to nurture and protect other animals in whatever ways we can.

# afterword

## The Ten Trusts

Many people think that to make a positive difference they have to do something "big." Maybe found an organization, raise a bunch of money, or save a species. They also sometimes assume that if they can't do something like that, it's not worth doing anything.

That's not true.

If one person helps just one animal—say, befriends an octopus or rescues a fish—that animal's life has been saved or improved. If every person on Earth did just one thing, that's eight billion animals with better lives.

And if we go through our lives performing small acts of kindness for animals, that becomes countless practical ways we have made the world better. Every individual matters, including ourselves.

The world's problems didn't arise in a day, and they can't be fixed in one. However, big, complex issues can slowly be improved if, every day, we stay positive and hopeful and do what we can.

In 2002, to help inspire people to become caretakers of animals and our planet, Marc and Jane Goodall coauthored the book *The Ten Trusts*. These "trusts" represent both a mindset and a call to action. Here they are:

One: Rejoice that we are part of the animal kingdom.

Two: Respect all life.

Three: Open our minds, in humility, to animals and learn from them.

Four: Teach our children to respect and love nature.

Five: Be wise stewards of life on Earth.

Six: Value and help preserve the sounds of nature.

Seven: Refrain from harming life in order to learn about it.

Eight: Have the courage of our convictions.

Nine: Praise and help those who work for animals and the natural world.

Ten: Act knowing we are not alone and live with hope.

In this book, we've shared a lot of information about the inner lives of animals and why they matter. We hope you've enjoyed reading it as much as we've enjoyed writing it. We hope we've piqued your curiosity to learn more.

We also hope we've inspired you to "get started" by doing whatever you can to help animals—both the nonhuman and human variety—as well as Earth, our shared home. We hope the examples of young people and adults taking action spark your own ideas about what to do: Study animals, care for them, raise your voice, make compassionate personal choices, join organizations, and build community. Jane Goodall liked to say, "Act locally, think globally." We agree.

There are countless ways to embody the Ten Trusts. While it's true that other animals can often suffer in silence, since they can't speak to us directly, empathy and observation allow us to understand how they feel and what they need.

However, it's important to acknowledge that taking action isn't always easy. It takes work, and sometimes others don't agree with what we believe or what we want to change. On the one hand, after advocating on behalf of animals his whole life, Marc is grateful that caring for animals is becoming more mainstream. Respecting and preserving our precious world is increasingly embraced as an urgent necessity. And yet these feelings are still not universal. Advocacy on behalf of animals and nature can still be disparaged and dismissed, and it's important not to be put off by those who disagree. Marc likes to say that helping animals is all about decency. It shouldn't be written off as "radical." So, when talking to people, he focuses on the positive changes he is seeking.

And if some people continue to disagree, Marc has learned that it's often better to ignore them than to argue. In essence, some people can feel threatened by compassion toward animals and Earth, but it's never wrong.

Our advice is to reflect on what feels right and most important to you. Then do whatever you feel called to do to help make the world a kinder place. Don't be discouraged by anyone because the world needs a lot more kindness, and animals depend on us as their lifeline or oxygen.

Animals have taught us a great deal: about responsibility, caring, forgiveness, and the value of deep friendship and love. Animals connect with us because we are feeling and passionate beings, and we embrace them for the same reasons.

Whenever we open our hearts to animals, we discover that many animals do the same with us.

Group portrait, including Marc, Jane, Rusty, and Mooch by Patrick McDonnell.

# acknowledgments

First and foremost, Marc thanks Jane Goodall, his long-time friend and colleague, for all that he learned from working closely with her on the Ethics Committee of the Jane Goodall Institute and on various books and articles. Her unyielding support of his own research and writing played a major part in his personal and professional life for more than twenty-five years. She will be forever missed by Marc and countless people around the world. Mary Lewis, VP and assistant to Dr. Goodall, was always there to help find Jane when she was on the road, as was Susana Name. Marc also thanks all of the wonderful people who contributed photographs and personal stories. A special thanks goes to award-winning Images of Nature photographer Thomas D. Mangelsen and his studio manager/editor Andrew Bennett.

Jeff expresses profound thanks to coauthor Marc Bekoff, whose research and advocacy inspired him to write about animals. Jeff's previous books owe a huge debt to Marc, and he's deeply honored to be his collaborator on this one. Thanks to Maryann Karinch for championing this book, as well as to the Armin Lear team for making it a reality. For their help reading early drafts and providing invaluable feedback, Jeff is deeply indebted to his Madison critique group—Judy, Elana, Kara, James, Tiffany, Eileen, and Jacqui—as well as to the following teachers and teens: Matt Daly and his daughter Brigid; Andrew Lutz and his daughter Katie; Linnea Hasegawa and her students Katherine and Sophia; and Noga Beer and two dozen of her seventh- and eighth-grade students at Red Oaks School. A shout out to the librarians at Morristown and Morris County is always necessary. And Jeff would never survive without his family's endless love and support. Thanks, D, J, M. This one's for you.

# select bibliography

This bibliography lists the main books used for research.
Source notes can be found at marcbekoff.com/love-in-their-hearts.


Bearzi, Maddalena. *Dolphin Confidential: Confessions of a Field Biologist.* University of Chicago Press, 2012.

Bearzi, Maddalena, and Craig B. Stanford. *Beautiful Minds: The Parallel Lives of Great Apes and Dolphins.* Harvard University Press, 2008.

Bekoff, Marc. *The Animal Manifesto: Six Reasons for Expanding Our Compassion Footprint.* New World Library, 2010.

———. *Animals Matter: A Biologist Explains Why We Should Treat Animals with Compassion and Respect.* Shambhala Publications, 2007.

———. *Dogs Demystified: An A–Z Guide to All Things Canine.* New World Library, 2023.

———. *The Emotional Lives of Animals, Revised Edition.* New World Library, 2007/2024.

———. *Rewilding Our Hearts: Building Pathways of Compassion and Coexistence.* New World Library, 2014.

———, editor. *The Smile of a Dolphin: Remarkable Accounts of Animal Emotions.* Discovery Books, 2000.

Bekoff, Marc, and Jessica Pierce. *The Animals' Agenda: Freedom, Compassion, and Coexistence in the Human Age*. Beacon Press, 2017.

———. *Unleashing Your Dog: A Field Guide to Giving Your Companion the Best Life Possible.* New World Library, 2019.

———. *Wild Justice: The Moral Lives of Animals*. University of Chicago Press, 2009.

Campbell, Jeff. *Daisy to the Rescue: True Stories of Daring Dogs, Paramedic Parrots, and Other Animal Heroes.* Zest Books, 2014.

———. *Glowing Bunnies!?: Why We're Making Hybrids, Chimeras, and Clones*. Lerner/Zest Books, 2022.

———. *Last of the Giants: The Rise and Fall of Earth's Most Dominant Species*. Zest Books, 2016.

de Waal, Frans. *Mama's Last Hug: Animal Emotions and What They Tell Us about Ourselves.* W. W. Norton & Co., 2019.

Godfrey-Smith, Peter. *Other Minds: The Octopus, the Sea, and the Deep Origins of Consciousness.* Farrar, Straus and Giroux, 2016.

Goodall, Jane. *The Chimpanzees of Gombe: Patterns of Behavior*. Belknap Press, 1986.

———. *In the Shadow of Man.* Mariner Books/Houghton Mifflin Harcourt, 1971/2010.

———. *Jane Goodall: 50 Years at Gombe*. Stewart, Tabori & Chang, 2010.

Goodall, Jane, and Marc Bekoff. *The Ten Trusts: What We Must Do to Care for the Animals We Love*. HarperOne, 2003.

Hargrove, John, with Howard Chua-Eoan. *Beneath the Surface: Killer Whales, SeaWorld, and the Truth Beyond Blackfish.* Palgrave Macmillan, 2015.

Hutto, Joe, *Touching the Wild: Living with the Mule Deer of Deadman Gulch.* Skyhorse Publishing, 2014.

Keim, Brandon. *Meet the Neighbors: Animal Minds and Life in a More-Than-Human World.* W. W. Norton, 2024.

King, Barbara J. *How Animals Grieve.* University of Chicago Press, 2013.

———. *Personalities on the Plate: The Lives & Minds of Animals We Eat.* University of Chicago Press, 2017.

Montgomery, Sy. *How to Be a Good Creature.* Houghton Mifflin Harcourt, 2018.

———. *The Soul of an Octopus.* Atria Books/Simon & Schuster, 2015.

Mustill, Tom. *How to Speak Whale: A Voyage into the Future of Animal Communication.* Grand Central Publishing, 2022.

O'Barry, Richard, with Keith Coulbourn. *Behind the Dolphin Smile.* Chapel Hill, NC: Algonquin Books of Chapel Hill, 1988.

O'Connell, Caitlin. *Wild Rituals: 10 Lessons Animals Can Teach Us about Connection, Community, and Ourselves.* Chronicle Prism, 2021.

Recio, Belinda. *When Animals Rescue: Amazing True Stories about Heroic and Helpful Creatures.* Skyhorse Publishing, 2020.

Safina, Carl. *Becoming Wild: How Animal Cultures Raise Families, Create Beauty, and Achieve Peace.* Henry Holt and Company, 2020.

———. *Beyond Words: What Animals Think and Feel.* Henry Holt and Company, 2015.

Skiff, Jennifer. *Rescuing Ladybugs: Inspirational Encounters with Animals That Changed the World.* New World Library, 2018.

# get started resources

Whether you want to learn more or do more, here are places to get started:

## Citizen Science Projects

These organizations provide lists of current citizen-science projects across the United States that need volunteers.

Association of Zoos & Aquariums, "Citizen Science": www.aza.org/citizen-science
CitizenScience.gov: www.citizenscience.gov
Cornell Lab of Ornithology, "Citizen Science": www.birds.cornell.edu/citizenscience
FrogWatch USA: www.akronzoo.org/frogwatch
NASA, "Citizen Science": https://science.nasa.gov/citizen-science
National Audubon Society, "Community Science": www.audubon.org/community-science
National Geographic Education, "Citizen Science Projects": https://education.nationalgeographic.org/resource/citizen-science-projects
SciStarter: https://scistarter.org
Society for Science, "Research at Home: Citizen Science": www.societyforscience.org/research-at-home/citizen-science
Zooniverse: www.zooniverse.org

## Advocacy and Taking Action

This is a select group of international, national, and regional groups that focus on animal advocacy and animal conservation and welfare.

Animal Equality: https://animalequality.org
Animal Legal Defense Fund: https://aldf.org
Animals Asia: https://www.animalsasia.org
Animal Welfare Institute: https://awionline.org
Born Free USA: https://www.bornfreeusa.org
Center for Biological Diversity: www.biologicaldiversity.org
Compassion in World Farming: https://www.ciwf.com
Fish Welfare Initiative: https://www.fishwelfareinitiative.org
The Humane League: https://thehumaneleague.org
In Defense of Animals: https://www.idausa.org
Institute for Humane Education: https://humaneeducation.org
Jane Goodall Institute: https://janegoodall.org
Maine Big Night: https://mainebignight.org
Mercy for Animals: https://mercyforanimals.org
National Audubon Society: www.audubon.org
Nature Conservancy: www.nature.org
Nonhuman Rights Project: www.nonhumanrights.org
NYC Bird Alliance: https://nycbirdalliance.org
People for the Ethical Treatment of Animals (PETA): www.peta.org
Project Coyote: https://projectcoyote.org
Roots & Shoots: https://rootsandshoots.org
Switch4Good: https://switch4good.org
World Wildlife Fund, "Educational Resources": www.worldwildlife.org/teaching-resources

## Books about Animals

Buchmann, Stephen. *What a Bee Knows: Exploring the Thoughts, Memories, and Personalities of Bees*. Island Press, 2023.

Bumann, George. *Eavesdropping on Animals: What We Can Learn from Wildlife Conversations*. Greystone Books, 2024.

Chakour, Vanessa. *Earthly Bodies: Embracing Animal Nature*. Penguin Life, 2024.

Cooke, Lucy. *Bitch: On the Female of the Species*. Basic Books, 2022.

Danovich, Tove. *Under the Henfluence: Inside the World of Backyard Chickens and the People Who Love Them*. Agate Publishing, 2023.

Despret, Vinciane. *What Would Animals Say If We Asked the Right Questions?*. Translated by Brett Buchanan. University of Minnesota Press, 2016.

Dugatkin, Lee. *The Principles of Animal Behavior*. University of Chicago Press, 2013.

Hein, Till. *The Curious World of Seahorses: The Life and Lore of a Marine Marvel*. Greystone Books, 2023.

Higgins, Jackie. *Sentient: How Animals Illuminate the Wonder of Our Human Senses*. Atria Books, 2022.

Kershenbaum, Arik. *Why Animals Talk: The New Science of Animal Communication*. Penguin Press, 2024.

Kimmerer, Robin Wall. *Braiding Sweetgrass: Indigenous Wisdom, Scientific Knowledge, and the Teachings of Plants*. Milkweed Editions, 2015.

Lihoreau, Mathieu. *What Do Bees Think About?*. Translated by Alison Duncan. Johns Hopkins University Press, 2024.

Masson, Jeffrey Moussaieff, and Susan McCarthy. *When Elephants Weep: The Emotional Lives of Animals*. Random House, 1996.

Monsó, Susana. *Playing Possom: How Animals Understand Death*. Princeton University Press, 2024.

Montgomery, Sy. *What the Chicken Knows: A New Appreciation of the World's Most Familiar Bird*. Atria Books, 2024.

Nelson, Ximena. *The Lives of Spiders: A Natural History of the World's Spiders*. Princeton University Press, 2024.

Roach, Mary. *Fuzz: When Nature Breaks the Law.* W. W. Norton, 2021.

Sapp, Merrill. *Knowing Wonder: An Elephant Story*. Chin Music Press, 2025.

Schlanger, Zoë. *The Light Eaters: How the Unseen World of Plant Intelligence Offers a New Understanding of Life on Earth*. Harper, 2024.

Schrefer, Eliot. *Queer Ducks (and Other Animals): The Natural World of Animal Sexuality.* Katherine Tegen Books, 2022.

Telkänranta, Helena. *The Mind of a Horse: Science Meets Comics.* Arador Publishing, 2024.

Yong, Ed. *An Immense World: How Animal Senses Reveal the Hidden Realms Around Us.* Random House, 2022.

Young, Rosamund. *The Wisdom of Sheep: Observation from a Family Farm.* Penguin Press, 2024.

Yunker, John, ed. *Writing for Animals: New Perspectives for Writers and Instructors to Educate and Inspire*. Ashland Creek Press, 2018.

# index

Note: Page references in *italics* refer to illustrative matter.


abuse, 88–91, 104, 117, 137–38. *See also* captivity of animals; research labs
accidental altruism, 193. *See also* altruism
accumulative rock throwing, 71–72
Ackerman, Jennifer, 26
Action for Nature's International Eco-Hero Youth Awards, 197
actions humans can take, 4–5; on animal laws and regulations, 137–40; for backyard wildlife, 150–53; citizen science, 33–37; compassionate conservation, 178–81; compassionate eating and shopping habits, 93–95; fighting for environmental rights, 197–98; harm reduction behavior, 8–9, 56–57, 93, 94–95, 138, 180, 205–9; humane education in the classroom, 55–57; O'Barry on, 117; resources for, 214–17; rewilding our hearts, 7, 205–6; unleashing pets, 75–76; youth-led climate lawsuits, 198; zoos and waterparks, 120–21. *See also* altruism; coexistence; Roots & Shoots program (Jane Goodall Institute)
adaptations, 22, 32, 87, 144
Adélie penguins, 8, 143–44
affection, 44, 76, 81, 127, 156, 158, 195. *See also* compassion; love
African gray parrots, 124–27
Alaska SeaLife Center, *59*
Alex (parrot), 124–27
altruism, 184–85, 206; by a cat, 185–86; by a dog, 183; by dolphins, 187–90; by humpback whales, 190–93; protecting sea life from fishing waste, 194–97, 199–200; by rats, 47. *See also* actions humans can take
Amboseli Elephant Research Project, 23–24
amphibians, 7, 151, 170
Andean bears, 180. *See also* bears
anger, 123–40
animal captivity. *See* captivity of animals
animal education in classrooms, 7, 9, 55–57
animal emotions, overview, 27–28. See also *names of specific animals and emotions*
animal escapes, 61–62, 66–69, 75
animal ethics. *See* ethology and ethologists
animal intelligence. *See* intelligence of animals
animal laws and regulations, 84, 137–40
animal personhood, 139–40
animal rights, 84, 137–40
animal sentience. *See* sentience of animals
animal testing on cosmetics, 94
animal training, 112–15, 132–36
animal welfare laws, 84, 137–40
Animals Asia, 88, 89
Antarctica, 8, 143–44
Anthropocene, 204
anthropodenial, 83. *See also* superiority complex of humans
anthropomorphism, 8, 82–83

ants, 6, 84, 86, 194
anxiety, 2, 78, 79, 107
apes. *See* bonobos; chimpanzees; orangutans
apology behaviors, 17, 19, 21, 53
aquariums: octopuses in, *59,* 60–64, 128; the problem with, 120–21. *See also* captivity of animals; waterparks; zoos
artificial insemination, 79. *See also* breeding programs
Asiatic black bears, *77,* 88–91
ASL (American Sign Language), 53–55, 67
ASPCA, 186
autism, 49–52, 185, 200
AWA (US Federal Animal Welfare Act), 137–38, 140
awe, 70–73

baboons, 22, 145–47
backyard wildlife, 150–53
Balcomb, Ken, 108
Balto (dog), *183*
Bartal, Inbal Ben-Ami, 47
Beach, Kat, 53
beach clean-ups, 198
Bear 399 (grizzly bear), *1,* 170–77, *178*
Bear 610 (grizzly bear), 172–73, 176
bear bile farming, 88–90
bear jams, 171, 173, *174,* 175–76
bears: Asiatic black bears and bear bile farming, *77,* 88–91; conservation efforts for, 180–81; grizzlies in Grand Teton National Park, *1,* 170–77, *178*; Marsican bears in Italy, 152
Bearzi, Maddalena, 3, 30, 43, 107–8
Beck, Benjamin B., 145–47
beekeeping, 181
bees, ii, 26–27, 86–87
Bekoff, Marc: early life of, 6–7; Goodall and, iii–iv, *9*; play research by, 8–9, 34; *The Ten Trusts,* iv, 9, 207–9; work of, iii–iv, v, 4–5, 65
Betsy (horse), 49–52
biocentric anthropomorphism, 83
bipedal swagger, 142
Birch, Jonathan, 84, 86
birds: Alex (parrot), 124–27; chicken behavior, 44–45; corvid mourning rituals, 104–5; crows, 26, 105; dolphin play with, 31; Jethro's story with, 42; penguins, 8, 143–44; play by, 26; protecting habitat for, 150–51; ravens, 22, 26, 105
Boal, Jean, 130
bobcats, 12
bonobos, 148
book drives, 197
boredom, 62, 66, 118, 134. *See also* captivity of animals; repetitive behavior
Born Free Foundation, 120
Borneo, 200–204
Borneo Orangutan Survival Foundation (BOSF), 201–2
bowing, 18–19, 22
breeding programs, 78–81, 121
Bronx Zoo, 121, 139
Brooke, Rylee, 197–98
Brookfield Zoo, 145
Browning, Ricou, 112
bubble play, 30
Buchmann, Stephen, 87
burial practices and animal behaviors, 99–105. *See also* grief; mourning
butterflies, 86

Campbell, Jeff, 4
canids, *141. See also* dogs
captivity effects, as term, 120. *See also* captivity of animals
captivity of animals: cows, 78–81; dolphins, 111–16; elephants, 120, 121, 139–40; escaping, 61–62, 66–69, 75; moon bears, 88–90; octopuses, *59,* 60–64, 127–30; orangutans, 54–55, 66–69; orcas (killer whales), 132–36; pigs, 118–19; the problem with, 120–21; Wemelsfelder on, 118. *See also* abuse; cruelty; freedom; research labs
cats, 12, *123,* 142, 185–86. *See also* lions
cephalopods, ii, *59,* 60–64, 84–85
cetaceans. *See* dolphins; orcas (killer whales); whales
Chantek (orangutan), 54–55, 67
chewing, 76
chickens, ii, 44–45, 138
child separation, 79–81
childhood inspirations, 4; Breanna Locke, 74; Camilla Fox, 92; Leilani Münter, 147; Maddalena Bearzi, 43; Marlon Reis, 193–94; Wendy Townsend, 169–70. *See also* play
chimpanzees, *39*; drumming by, 71–72; Goodall's work with, iii, iv, 33, 70–71, 72–73, 74, 109–11, 159–64;

grief by, 108–9; love and affection among, 109–11, 159–64; play of, 22, 163; rain dance by, 70–71; social emotions of, 124, 142; viewing the sunset, 73; Washoe's language learning, 53; waterfall worship by, 72–73
citizen science, 33–37. *See also* fieldwork
Clark, Susan, 175
classroom education, 7, 9, 55–57
cockroaches, 86
coexistence, 150, 151–53, 170–76, 180, 204–5
cognitive ethology, defined, 5, 32. *See also* ethology and ethologists
Collective Fashion Justice, 94
commitment, 156
companion animals (pets), 75–76, 86. See also *names of specific species*
compassion, 4, 39; of apes, 53–55; of horses, 49–52; of rats, 47. *See also* affection; empathy; love
compassion footprint, 93–95
compassionate conservation, as discipline, 32
compassionate eating, 74, 92, 93–94
compassionate shopping, 94–95
confinement. *See* captivity of animals
conscientious omnivores, 94
conservation, 48, 65, 120, 150–51, 178–81, 193, 202–4
consoling gestures, 156. *See also* compassion; grief
contempt, 123–40
cooperation, 20–22
corvids, 22, 26, 104–5
cosmetics industry, 94
*The Cove* (film), 117, 147
Cow #6490, 78–81
cows, ii, 78–81
coydogs, 8
coyotes, *8,* 142–43, 152–53
crabs, 84
crickets, 86
crisis of coexistence, 204–5. *See also* coexistence
criteria for animal sentience, 84–85, 86. *See also* sentience of animals
crows, 26, 105
cruelty, 88–90. *See also* captivity of animals
crush cages, 89–90
crustaceans, 84–85
curiosity, 33, 59–76

dairy cows, 78–81
Danovich, Tove, 45
Darwin, Charles, 28, 33, 97–98
David Greybeard (chimpanzee), iii, 159–64
de Waal, Frans, 22, 33, 70, 83, 142
debeaking, 138
Decety, Jean, 47
declawing, 138
deer, 164–69
dehorning, 79, 138
depression, 87, 98, 111, 115–16, 120. *See also* grief; sadness
devotion, 28, 63, 107, 133, 156, 170–71, 173, 177
Dews, Peter, 129
diet and compassion, 74, 92, 93–94
diseases, 79, 183
disgust, 28, 124. *See also* anger
dissection of animals, 7, 9, 55–56
distress, 84–87
distributed intelligence, 61
do no harm, as principle, 180. *See also* harm reduction behavior
dogs: Balto, *183*; Darwin on, 98; emotions of, 1–2, 82, 142; freedom and, 75–76; Jethro, 16–17, 35, 37, 40–42; legal rights of, 139; play by, 16–20, 22; rights and protections of, 137; Rusty, ii, iii. *See also* companion animals (pets)
Dolphin Project, 117, 147
dolphins: in captivity, 111–16, 120; legal rights of, 139; mourning behavior of, 107–8; in Pakistan, 199–200; play by, 29–31; shark attacks and, 187–90. *See also* orcas (killer whales)
Douglas-Hamilton, Iain, 143
ducks, 104
Dyke, Mark, 40

eating disorders, 115
echolocation, 114, 115, 199–200
economics of dairy farming, 81
elephants, *15, 24, 97*; in captivity, 120, 121, 139–40; emotions of, 98–99; fieldwork with, 143; legal rights on, 139; love emotions by, 156–59; mourning of, 99–103; play by, 23–24
emotional contagion, 27

emotions, overview, 27–28. See also *names of specific emotions and animals*
empathy: of apes, 53–55; defined, 39–40, 83; early scientific thought on, iii, 4; of horses, 49–52; importance of, 3, 4, 6–7; of rats, 47. *See also* compassion
empathy gap, 4
Endris, Todd, 187–90
equine therapy, 49–52
escaping animals, 61–62, 66–69, 75. *See also* captivity of animals
ethical fashion, 94–95
ethograms, 34, 36
Ethologists for the Ethical Treatment of Animals (organization), 9
ethology and ethologists, iii, iv, 3, 5, 8, 32–33, 205
Etosha National Park, *11*, 13–16, 23, 105–6, 156–57
euthanasia, 121, 171, 175

fairness, 17, 20–22
farming, 48, 78–81, 119, 138, 198–99. *See also* livestock predation
fashion and fashion industry, 94–95
fieldwork, 8, 142–44. *See also* citizen science; *names of specific scientists*
filial love, 156
Fischer, Bob, 87
fish, 34, 40, 85, 138
fishing lines and sea life entanglements, 194–97, 199–200
Fishlock, Vicky, 23–24
fitness, as term, 184
five freedoms, 138. *See also* freedom
flies, 86
Flint (chimpanzee), 109–10, 163
*Flipper* (movies and TV shows), 111–14, 116
Flo (chimpanzee), 109–11, 163
"four golden rules of play," 21. *See also* play
four principles of compassionate conservation, 180. *See also* conservation
Fox, Camilla, 92, 94
Fox, Michael W., 8
foxes, 34, 105
freedom, 138; captive animal escapes, 61–62, 66–69, 75; of companion animals, 75–76. *See also* captivity of animals
Freya (orca), 132–36
friendship, 156, 158–59
frogs, 151
frustration, 123–40
Fu Manchu (orangutan), 68
funeral rituals and animal behaviors, 99–105. *See also* mourning
fur industry, 94
Future of Nature Awards, 197

Galpayage, Samadi, 26
giant Pacific octopuses, *59*, 60–63, 128
Gillespie, Kathryn, 78
giraffes, 25, 107
goats, 22
Godfrey-Smith, Peter, 61
Golden Rule(s), 21
Goliath (chimpanzee), 160, 162
Gombe National Park, iii, 70–71, 109, 159–64
Goodall, Jane, i–v, *73*; Bekoff and, iii–iv, *9*; chimpanzee work by, iii, iv, 33, 70–71, 72–73, 109–11, 159–64; *In the Shadow of Man,* 110, 161; *The Ten Trusts,* iv, 9, 207–9; on trust, 159–60, 163, 168. *See also* Jane Goodall Institute; Roots & Shoots program (Jane Goodall Institute)
Grand Teton National Park, *1,* 8, 142, 170–77, *178*
Grandin, Temple, 50–51
grasshoppers, 86
gratitude, 5, 183–206
great apes. *See* bonobos; chimpanzees; orangutans
greeting behavior, *11,* 23, 156–59
grief, 98–111, 156, 173. *See also* burial practices and animal behaviors; mourning; sadness; suffering
grizzly bears, 170–77, *178*
grooming behavior, *11,* 163, 167
guilt, 28, 141, 142, 181

*habeas corpus,* 139
Håkansson, Emma, 94–95
Happy (elephant), 121, 139
Hargrove, John, 132–33, 134–36
harm, 55–57, 88–90, 180. *See also* abuse; pain and suffering; self-harm
harm reduction behavior, 8–9, 56–57, 93, 94–95, 138, 180, 205–9. *See also* actions humans can take
Hawai'i, 197–98
hazing, 175
hedgehogs, 180

hope, i, iv, 5, 64–65, 90, 91, 207–9
Horse Boy Method, 49–52
horses, 49–52
humane education in the classroom, 55–57
Humane Slaughter Act, 138
humpback whales, 190–93
hunting, 48, 178
Hutto, Joe and Leslye, 164–69

Iguana Specialist Group, 169
iguanas, *86,* 169–70
*In the Shadow of Man* (Goodall), 110, 161
inadvertent altruism, 193. *See also* altruism
India, 151, 152
indigenous ecological knowledge, 151–52
individuality of emotions, 28, 33, 45, 48, 76, 78, 91, 120, 144, 159
individuals matter, as principle, 180, 207
Indonesia, 200–204
Indus dolphins, 199–200
insects, ii, 26–27, 86–87
intelligence of animals, ii. 29, 60–61, 78, 98, 104, 168
International Union for Conservation of Nature, 169
invasive species, 179, 180
Isaacson, Rowan, 49–52
Isaacson, Rupert, 49–52
Italy, 152

Jaicks, Hannah, 54
Jane Goodall Institute, v, 5. *See also* Roots & Shoots program (Jane Goodall Institute)
Jasper (moon bear), *77,* 88, 90–91
Jawwad, Romaan, 199
jealousy, 28, 83, 136, 141, 144–45, 149–50
Jefferson, Sam, 151
Jensen, Joe, 188
Jethro (dog), 16–17, 35, 37, 40–42
joy, 1, 17, 19, 22, 27. *See also* laughter; play
joy jumps, 22

Kanzi (bonobo), 148–50
Kathy (dolphin), 112, 113, 114, 115, 116–17
keas, 26
Keim, Brandon, 151
Ken Allen (orangutan), 69
Kenya, 23–24, 143, 198–99
Kessler, Janet, 152
killer whales. *See* orcas (killer whales)
King, Barbara, 104

language and animal emotions, iii, 8, 48, 82–83
laughter, 25. *See also* joy; play
laws and regulations on animals, 84, 137–40
Leakey, Louis, 33
Leikam, Bill, 34
lexical elision, 125
lexigrams, 148–50
Lion Lights, 198–99
lions, *13,* 14–16, 120, *155. See also* cats
livestock predation, 181, 198–99. *See also* farming
lobsters, 84
Locke, Breanna, 74
longing, 80–81
Lorenz, Konrad, 32
love, 81, 155–81. *See also* affection; compassion
loyalty, 156

macaws, 26
magpies, 104–5
Maine Big Night, 151
Mangelsen, Tom, 170–74, 177
manta rays, 196–97
Manta Trust, 196
Marineland, 132
Marsican bears, 152
Mason, Peggy, 47
Masson, Jeffrey Moussaieff, 80, 117–18, 119
mastitis, 79
maternal love, 109–10, 156. *See also* love
matriarchal societies, 109–10, 132–33, 135, 157, 170
May, Brian, 82
McGreevy, Paul, 76
Miami Seaquarium, 112, 116
mice, 34, 137
microactivism, 65. *See also* actions humans can take
Miles, Lyn, 54–55, 67
minding animals, as concept, 6–7
mirror test, 44, 139
mobbing behavior, 190, 192
Mogil, Jeffrey, 47
Monsó, Susana, 103
Montgomery, Sy, 44–45, 60–64
Moon Bear Rescue Centre, 88, 90
moon bears, *77,* 88–91
moral disgust, 124
morality, 17, 21, 22
Moskito, James, 195
mosquitoes, 86

Moss, Cynthia, 99–100, 139
moths, 86
mourning, 99–108, 173. *See also* burial practices and animal behaviors; grief
Movement Method, 52
mule deer, 164–69
Münter, Leilani, 147
Mushara waterhole, Etosha National Park, 13–16, 23, 105–6
mutual caretaking, 156

Nakashima, Satoshi, 47
Namibia, *11,* 13–16
natural selection theory, 191
nautilus, 84
necking, 25
New England Aquarium, 60, 62
New Zealand, 117–18
Nonhuman Rights Project (NhRP), 139
numbering animals, iii, 48
NYC Bird Alliance, 151

O'Barry, Ric, 112–17, 147
objective *vs.* subjective language, iii, 8, 48, 82–83, 121
Ocean Conservation Society, 43
Oceanic Preservation Society, 147
O'Connell, Caitlin: on chimpanzees, 71–72; on elephants, 24, 156–58; on giraffes, 25; on lions, 13–16; on zebras, 23, 105–6; on zoos, 121
Octavia (octopus), 60–63
octopuses: in captivity, *59,* 60–64, 127–30; physical description of, ii; sentience of, 84
Omaha Zoo, 68
operant conditioning, 112
optimism, i, 5. *See also* hope
orangutans, 54–55, 66–69, 201–4
orcas (killer whales): in captivity, 120, 132–36; dialects of, 135; humpback whales defense against, 190–93; mourning by, 108; play by, 29, 30–31; sleeping, 115. *See also* dolphins

Paidia (lion), 14–16
pain and suffering: Bekoff on, 7; of cows, 79–81; measuring sentience and, 84–87; of moon bears, 88–91; of rats, 46–47. *See also* abuse; captivity of animals; grief; harm reduction behavior
Pakistan, 199–200
Panbanisha (bonobo), 148, 149–50
Panksepp, Jaak, 25
pant-hoot, 71–72, 73
parrots, 26, 124–27
peaceful coexistence, as principle, 180. *See also* coexistence
penguins, 8, 143–44
Pepperberg, Irene, 124–27
personhood of animals, 139–40
PETA (People for the Ethical Treatment of Animals), 94
pets, 75–76, 86, 201. See also *names of specific species*
Pettorano sul Gizio, Italy, 152
pheromones, 19
Philadelphia Zoo, 108–9
physical closeness, 156
pigs, 117–19
Pitman, Robert, 190–93
plants, 131–32
Plastics Project, 198
play, 11–12; by bears, 174; by bees, 26–27; Bekoff's study of, 8–9, 34; by birds, 26; by chimpanzees, 22, 163; by dogs, 16–20; by dolphins, 29–31; by elephants, 23–24; fairness in, 20–22; by giraffes, 25; by lions, *13,* 14–16; by orcas (killer whales), 31; by penguins, 144; by rats, 25; the what and why of, 19–20, 22; by zebras, 23. *See also* childhood inspirations; joy; laughter
play inhibition, 19
pleasure, 156
pneumonia, 164
Pollan, Michael, 94
Poole, Joyce, 100, 102, 139
pranking, 29, 31, 142–44. *See also* escaping animals
pride, 31, 141–42
Project Coyote, 92
Promise to Our Keiki program, 197–98
protectiveness, 156
PTSD (post-traumatic stress disorder), 87

quiet emotions, 119

rabbits, 8, 41–42
rain, 55, 70–71, 78
rainforest protection, 202
raking, 135
rats, 25, 46–47, 137, 140
ravens, 22, 26, 105
reciprocal social bonds, 156

Reis, Marlon, 193–94
Reiss, Diana, 30, 31
relaxation, *77*
relocation of wildlife, 171, 175–76, 179
repetitive behavior, 49, 89, 107, 112, 118. *See also* boredom; captivity of animals
reptiles, 86
research labs, 46–47, 48, 54, 129, 137, 140, 201. *See also* captivity of animals
resentment, 146–47
resident orcas, 192. *See also* orcas (killer whales)
resource sharing, 149–50, 156
respect, 156
rewilding education, 55
rewilding our hearts, 7, 205–6
rhinos, 22, 120
rights and regulations on animals, 84, 137–40
Robinson, Jill, 88–91
rodents, 25, 34, 137
role-reversing, 19, 21
romantic love, 156. *See also* love
Roots & Shoots program (Jane Goodall Institute), iii–iv, v, 5, 9, 64–65, 74
Rusty (dog), ii, iii

sadness, 53, 54–55, 97–121. *See also* depression; grief
Safer Nets for Healthier Oceans project, 199–200
Safina, Carl, 26, 30, 73, 133, 159
Samburu National Reserve, 143
San Diego Zoo, 69
San Francisco, California, 152
Sato, Nobuya, 47
Savage-Rumbaugh, Sue, 148–50
scents, 19, 35, 137
Schlanger, Zoë, 131–32
scuba diving, 195–97
seahorses, 85
sea-life parks. *See* aquariums
Seattle Aquarium, 128
SeaWorld, *134*
self-awareness, 35, 37, 87, 114, 139
self-handicapping, 19, 21
self-harm, 115, 118. *See also* harm; suicide
selflessness, 184
Semenggoh Nature Reserve, *201*
sentience of animals, ii, 2, 4, 84–87, 177
sentience of plants, 131–32
Shambala Publications, 74
shame, 28, 141, 142, 149
sharks, 187–90
sheep, 43, 92, 94
Sheldrake, Daphne, 103
shopping and compassion, 94–95
shrimp, 84
Siberian husky, *183*
silliness, 23–24, 90. *See also* play
singing, 118, 119
sixth extinction, 178–79
smell, 35, 137
Smits, Willie, 200–204
Sneddon, Lynne, 85
sniff experiment, 35, 36, 37
social play. *See* play
Society for the Study of Ethics & Animals, 87
sounds, 115
squids, 84
standing, *178*
stereotypic behaviors, 118
Stevens, Guy, 196
stimulus-and-response technique, 112
stress, 79, 87. *See also* anxiety
subjective *vs.* objective language, iii, 8, 48, 82–83, 121
suffering, 78, 84–87, 119. *See also* abuse; captivity of animals; grief; harm reduction behavior
sugar palms, 202
suicide, 117. *See also* self-harm
Sumatra, 202
superiority complex of humans, 4, 43, 99, 137–38, 204–5. *See also* anthropodenial
"surplus animals," 121

Tahlequah (killer whale), 108
Taiji dolphin hunts (Japan), 117
tail docking, 79
Tanzania, 33, 159
taste, 62
*The Ten Trusts* (Bekoff and Goodall), iv, 9, 207–9
tenderness, 156
termites, 86
tickling, 25
Tinbergen, Niko, 32
tolerance, 5, 150–53. *See also* coexistence
tools, making and use of, 148, 149, 159
Townsend, Wendy, 169–70

traditional Chinese medicine, 88
transient orcas, 192. *See also* orcas (killer whales)
trauma, 88–91
Travers, Bill, 120
Tribelhorn, Gunnar, 34
trunk-to-mouth ritual, 156–58
trust, 160–61; animal-animal, 17, 23, 156; animal-human, 41, 50, 91, 114, 158, 197; Goodall on, 9, 159–60, 163, 168, 207–9; human-human, 56; social bonds through, 20. See also *The Ten Trusts* (Bekoff and Goodall)
Turere, Richard, 198

unintended altruism, 193. *See also* altruism
United Kingdom, 84
universality of emotions, 2, 22, 28, 32–33, 156
University of Tennessee—Chattanooga, 67
unleashing pets, 75–76. *See also* pets
US Federal Animal Welfare Act (AWA), 137–38, 140

value all wildlife, as principle, 180
VanDenbos, Dennis, 172
vegetarianism and veganism, 74, 92, 93–94, 147
Velez-Liendo, Ximena, 180–81
voles, 19
von Frisch, Karl, 32

Warwick, Clifford, 86
Washoe (chimpanzee), 53
wasps, 86
waterfall dance, 72
waterparks: dolphins in, 111–16; orcas (killer whales) in, 132–36; the problem with, 120–21. *See also* aquariums; captivity of animals; zoos
Weil, Zoe, 76
welfare *vs.* well-being, 138. *See also* laws and regulations on animals
Wemelsfelder, Françoise, 118–19
whales, 190–95
wild justice, 22. *See also* morality
wildlife corridors, 151, 176
Wilkinson, Todd, 175, 177
Wise, Steve, 139
Wittemyer, George, 143
wolves, 8, 22, 65, 92, *141,* 180
wonder, 70–73
wool, 94
worry, 78, 142. *See also* anxiety
Wrede, Bastian, 65
Würsig, Bernd, 31

Yellowstone region, 170–76
youth-led climate lawsuits, 198. *See also* actions humans can take

zebrafish, 85
zebras, *11,* 23, 105–6
Zoo Atlanta, 54–55, 67
zoochosis, 120
zoomies, 18
zoos: baboons in, 145–47; chimpanzees in, 108–9; Happy (elephant) at, 139; orangutans in, 54–55, 66–69; the problem with, 120–21. *See also* aquariums; captivity of animals; waterparks
zoothanasia, 121

# about the authors

Marc Bekoff is professor emeritus of Ecology and Evolutionary Biology at the University of Colorado, Boulder. He has won many awards for his research and writing, including a Guggenheim Fellowship and the Exemplar Award from the Animal Behavior Society. He writes regularly for *Psychology Today* and has published more than thirty books, including *The Emotional Lives of Animals* and numerous scientific and popular essays. Visit marc-bekoff.com.

Jeff Campbell has written three books of young adult nonfiction: *Daisy to the Rescue* (an IPPY Gold Medal winner), *Last of the Giants*, and *Glowing Bunnies!?*, which was named a "Best Book for Teens 2023" by the New York Public Library and was an SCBWI Golden Kite Award finalist. Formerly a Lonely Planet travel writer, he's also a longtime book editor and writing teacher, helps run KidFest with the Morristown Festival of Books, practices yoga, and enjoys the occasional acting gig. Visit jeffcampbellbooks.com.

www.ingramcontent.com/pod-product-compliance
Lightning Source LLC
LaVergne TN
LVHW081325110826
845149LV00007B/1605
* 9 7 8 1 9 6 8 9 1 9 3 0 6 *